Theo-
logy
&
Life

THEOLOGY AND LIFE SERIES

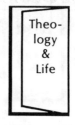

Volume 8

Contributors

Stephen Duffy
    Associate Professor of Systematic Theology, Loyola
    University New Orleans

Avery Dulles, S.J.
    Professor of Theology, The Catholic University of
    America

George Lindbeck
    Pitkin Professor of Historical Theology, Yale University

Gregory Baum
    Professor of Theology and Religious Studies, St.
    Michael's College in the University of Toronto

Francine Cardman
    Associate Professor of Historical Theology, Weston
    School of Theology

Vatican II
Open Questions and New Horizons

By

Stephen Duffy
Avery Dulles, S.J.
George Lindbeck
Gregory Baum
Francine Cardman

Editor:

Gerald M. Fagin, S.J.

Michael Glazier, Inc.
Wilmington, Delaware

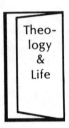

Theo-
logy
&
Life

ABOUT THE EDITOR:

Gerald M. Fagin, S.J., received his doctorate in theology from the University of St. Michael's College. He is Chairperson of the Religious Studies Department at Loyola University in New Orleans. Among his publications is *The Holy Spirit* (Volume 3 of *The Message of the Fathers of the Church* series published by Michael Glazier, Inc.), co-authored with J. Patout Burns, S.J.

BX
1751.2
.V345 / 49,373

First published in 1984 by Michael Glazier, Inc., 1723 Delaware Avenue, Wilmington, Delaware 19806 • Distributed outside the U.S., Canada and Philippines by Dominican Publications, St. Saviour's, Dublin 1, Ireland • ©1984 by Loyola University, New Orleans. All rights reserved. • Library of Congress Card Catalog Number: 83-82665 • International Standard Book Numbers: Theology and Life Series, 0-89453-295-2; Vatican II, 0-89453-366-5 (Michael Glazier, Inc.); 0-907271-21-9 (Dominican Publications) • Cover design by Lillian Brulc • Typography by Susan Pickett • Printed in the United States of America

CONTENTS

"The danger is that people will not *seek* any more, but will simply explore the inexhaustible warehouse of Vatican II. This will simply open a post-Vatican era, as once there was a post-Tridentine era. It would be a betrayal of *aggiornamento* to think it has been fixed once and for all in the texts of Vatican II." *Yves Congar, O. P.*

PREFACE

The years since Vatican II have been a time of radical change and theological ferment in the life of the Christian community. They have been years of excitement, of change, of hope and new life, but also years of disappointments and confusion, of new questions and fewer answers. The Council stimulated a great deal of discussion and reflection, but there remain many unresolved issues, many doctrinal and pastoral questions still to be explored.

This book collects a series of papers by five prominent theologians who have been actively involved in the interpretation and implementation of the decrees of Vatican II. The paper by Stephen Duffy was presented at a regional meeting of the College Society in New Orleans. The papers by Avery Dulles, George Lindbeck, Gregory Baum, and Francine Cardman were presented at Vatican II — Twenty Years After, a conference sponsored by the Department of Religious Studies of Loyola University in New Orleans in cooperation with the Albert Biever Memorial Lecture Series. The papers are presented here with necessary revisions for publication.

As their titles indicate, the papers deal with some of the major agenda items that have developed from the Council. They discuss the impact and implications of the Council and the work that remains to be done. The Afterword is the substance of a homily preached at the final liturgy of the

Vatican II Conference. In a more exhortatory style, it is an invitation to trust in the promise and respond to the challenge of Vatican II.

A special word of thanks to Dr. Andrew Macdonald, chairperson of the Guest Lecturers Committee and to the faculty of the Religious Studies Department at Loyola University in New Orleans. Their cooperation and hard work and the support of many other colleagues made the Conference on Vatican II a success and the publication of these papers a possibility.

Gerald M. Fagin, S.J.
Loyola University
New Orleans, Louisiana

CATHOLICISM'S SEARCH FOR A NEW SELF-UNDERSTANDING
Stephen Duffy

I. Introduction

What is being played out in contemporary Catholic life is the effort to come to terms with modernity. By modernity I refer to a complex of post Enlightenment cultural developments. A new consciousness has imposed itself on increasing numbers of people. Science, technology, industrialization, urbanization, social and psychological analyses, critical history, new philosophies, all mark a radical sundering from the ancient and medieval worlds in which Catholicism was shaped. Throughout the 19th century there were individuals and movements which struggled mightily to positively though not uncritically relate Catholicism to the new consciousness. There were, e.g., the Tübingen school of theology and the historical school of Munich under Döllinger. Nonetheless, Catholicism grew progressively negative and defensive as the century wore on. The modernist crisis at the turn of our century was born of the effort of another group of Catholic thinkers to realistically face the same issue. The official church, unappreciative of their adventurous ideas, reacted rigorously against them. The problem, however, would not go away. Approaching mid-20th century, thinkers like Adam, Guardini, Rahner,

Von Balthasar, Chenu, de Lubac, and Congar slowly, and often at great personal pain, brought Catholic thought to an encounter with modernity. In this context, Vatican II's sudden call for dialogue with modernity and *aggiornamento* proved far more complex and significant than many thought. Today the abandonment of conciliar themes by numerous theologians is, paradoxically, a response to that very call.

The turmoil into which Vatican II thrust Roman Catholicism is often attributed to the suddenness of its reform. It may also be attributed to the fact that Catholic consciousness held no paradigms of reform which could assimilate what it began to experience in the conciliar and post conciliar period.[1] Nor did the Council provide any systematic theoretical foundation for its pervasive theme, *aggiornamento*. The Council's decrees were committee compositions, born of compromise, marked by ambiguity, and often reluctantly acceptable to all and passionately loved by few. Technical theological language was avoided at the price of precision and coherence. Moved by pastoral concerns, the documents are characterized more by the desire to appeal to the affective priorities of all persons of good will than by the intention of responding to a need for theory.

Vatican II, however, did not by itself launch Christianity, nor even Catholicism, into a new era. The new era was already well under way. World War II is the watershed, not Vatican II. What the Council did was to legitimate certain progressive currents in Roman Catholic life and thought which strove to shift the course Catholicism had steered from Trent through Vatican II. In so doing the Council ignited the hope that Catholicism and the contemporary world could come to live in creative interaction. Roman Catholicism was embarked on a course leading to a new understanding of itself and of Christianity. The primary move was in ecclesiology. The *Constitution on the Church* is the most thoroughly prepared conciliar document and it is pivotal. In this document, in the *Decree on Ecumenism*, and

[1]J. O'Malley, "Reform, Historical Consciousness, and Vatican II's Aggiornamento," *Theological Studies* 32 (1971) 573-601.

in the *Constitution on the Church in the Modern World*, the ecclesiology of the Council engages in four basic shifts in focus that together constitute a program of decentralization or de-Romanization, and de-Westernization. These four shifts are from the papacy to the episcopal college, from the heirarchy to the laity, from Roman Catholic Christianity to the other christian churches, and from the christian church to the world.

II. *What the Council Mandated*

FROM PAPACY TO EPISCOPACY: COLLEGIALITY AND PLURALISM

Vatican I in no way altered Tridentine Catholicism. It reinforced it, for it concentrated magisterial, jurisdictional, and sacramental power in the papacy. In the late 19th century and the first half of the 20th century Roman Catholic ecclesiology treated at length of papal prerogatives. The pyramidal image of Roman Catholicism was in vogue, with attention fixed on the point of the pyramid from whence descended to the rest of the Church all truth, authority, and life. A papacy forced to relinquish monarchical power in the political sphere through loss of papal states, invoked unparalleled power in the spiritual domain. Roman Catholic ecclesiology up to mid-20th century reflects this. Papal claims to absolute jurisdiction in doctrinal, liturgical, and institutional matters went unchallenged.

Now it had been the intention even of Vatican I to place the papacy within the context of the whole episcopate. Given the state of 19th century ecclesiology it may be a blessing that its work was aborted. The contextualization of the papacy and its concomitant limitation was left to Vatican II. What it claims is that the apostles were established as a college with Peter at its head, that by divine institution the bishops succeed the Apostles, that there exists now an episcopal college with the pope as its head.[2] What seems signifi-

[2] *Lumen Gentium*, n.20.

cant here is that this collective authority of the college precedes the particular authority of any individual member, including its head. It is not the sum total of a pooled authority but the sharing of one, unified authority of a corporate body. All authority does not rest initially with a pope who doles it out to his delegates, the bishops.[3] The authority of the head may not be less than that of the whole, yet he exercises it not in isolation but as the head of a body, as one with his colleagues. The most characteristic expression of corporate authority is found in the ecumenical council. And historically, it has been by this voice that the Church's most significant pronouncements have always been made.

The upshot of all this, in theory, if not in practice, is a church committed to collegiality, to a corresponsibility which limits an autocratic papacy and curia, and to the autonomy of the local bishop and his church. As a member of the episcopal college the bishop shares in responsibility for the government and doctrine of the universal *Catholica*. As head of a college the bishop of Rome must provide leadership for the *Catholica* in collaboration and consultation with his fellow bishops. On the other hand, because the bishops are not vicars of the Roman Pontiff and do not receive authority from him, they and their churches, local and regional, retain a certain independence which, at least in theory, grounds the possibility of a healthy pluralism within the universal church. Thus, the Council introduced democratic elements into the life of the Church and a dialogical structure which can make for a decentralization and a de-Romanization.

FROM HIERARCHY TO PEOPLE: A CHALLENGE TO THE PYRAMIDAL MODEL

The Council introduced long neglected images of the Church ("people of God," "family," "prophetic community," etc.) alongside the classic political and hierarchical models, thereby challenging the control and appropriate-

---

[3]*Ibid.,* n. 27.

ness of the latter. Attention is redirected to Christians-in-community and away from the church-as-religious-organization. Because imagery plays a crucial role in the perception of social reality, the council's shift to personalist and organic images is of great ecclesiological significance.[4] Identification of the Church with the people who compose the community of faith directs ecclesiology away from the narrow vision of Vatican I's *De Ecclesia* and counteracts a centuries old use of "the church" to signify official levels or a personified abstraction. Collegiality, democratic procedures, and the possibility of pluralism are mandated across the board. The impact is little short of revolutionary.

The historical evolution of faith and experience rather than abstract categorizing now becomes the dominant logos to structure reflection about ecclesial life, not hierarchical authority. The *sensus fidelium* and reception assume new prominence as criteria of adequate theological reflection and of polity. Previous conciliar and papal doctrinal formulations become less dominant. Orthopraxis takes on renewed importance in regard to orthodoxa. As the cultic and secular life and experience of Christians is given prominence as a locus theologicus the social sciences may achieve increasing integration into ecclesiology. Finally, the laity have as a result increasingly asserted their rightful place in the ministry of the church.[5] Many diverse forms of service have come to be performed by persons not liturgically ordained to official pastorate. For that reason they were not considered strictly ministry; yet the existential reality has been a genuine exercise of Christian ministry.[6] This phe-

---

[4]A. Dulles, *Models of the Church* (New York: Doubleday, 1974).

[5]B. Cooke, "The Church: Catholic and Ecumenical," *Theology Today* 36 (1979) 363.

[6]The danger here is a reclericalization of the Church in that so many ministries of the laity are focused more on church and eucharist and less on "more secular" concerns. We might also note that the post-conciliar phenomenon of the lay theologian in a university arena is bound to impart to the theological enterprise advantages unknown when theology was done only by clerics and largely in the seminary context. On the relationship of diverse contexts or publics to theology cf. D. Tracy, *The Analogical Imagination* (New York: Crossroad, 1981).

nomenon, coupled with the clergy's identity crisis, has forced a reappraisal of the nature and grounds of christian ministry and beyond that of the relation between charism and structure.

Considering the first and second shifts together, it is clear that Vatican II endorsed a redistribution of power and a polycentric authority structure. It recognizes the need for a balancing of diverse centers of initiative within the system — the international Synod of bishops, national hierarchies, presbyteral Senates, diocesan and parish councils, and a variety of lay organizations. In a word it allows for the pluralism of a democratic republicanism, a polymorphic church.

FROM ROMAN CATHOLICISM TO CHRISTIAN CHURCHES: THE RELATIVIZATION OF CATHOLICISM

After the first seven ecumenical councils, successive general councils have sanctioned a progressive contraction of Christianity to one of its constitutive traditions, first the Western (Constantinople IV, Lateran V), then Western-Roman from Trent on. With Vatican I this tendency was so radicalized that since then some have concluded that the very possibility of celebrating a truly ecumenical council is, for Catholicism, an impossibility. But the conciliar Decree on Ecumenism *Unitatis Redintegratio* was a quantum leap and light years ahead of any previous Roman Catholic pronouncement on ecumenism. It is also theologically more advanced than anything issued from Rome on ecumenism since the Council.

In its acknowledgement that membership in the Church extends beyond the Roman Catholic community and includes all who are united to Christ in baptism, the Council made it imperative that Catholics expand their perception of the Church so as to embrace the traditions and the present reality of the other Christian communities. Ecumenism is not optional for ecclesiology. The either/or answer to the question of the true church yields to a more or less. Immediately in the wake of this change of course follows an array of hard questions. What is required for a Christian community to be true Church? What are the limits to a bewildering pluralism in doctrine, liturgy, and polity? To what extent is the Church's life bound to agencies and structures (e.g., episcopacy) always deemed necessary by Catholics to its very existence?

In the past two decades ecumenism has grown beyond the simple notion of the reunion of Christians. Beginning with Vatican II's *Nostra Aetate* the concern became the relation of faith as found in Judaism or Islam or the Eastern relig-ions to the faith of Christians. New Testament studies furthered the urgency of the question by showing that the Christian Church cannot identify itself as the kingdom. The Church may in some way pertain to the kingdom, but the reign of God in human lives transcends by far the social boundaries of the Christian Church. Again, all this severely strains traditional views and feelings about the Church as the unique guardian of revelation and ordinary mediator of salvation, for Christians are increasingly conscious of the role the high religions of the world have played as ways to fulfillment for countless numbers. The uniqueness of the Church is, of course, inextricably rooted in the uniqueness of Jesus; hence ecclesiology is inseparable from develop-ments in Christology and soteriology.[7] And hence the recent spate of Christologies and texts on Catholicism as a nervous and/or questioning post-conciliar community casts about to maintain its identity and to legitimate its claims to abso-lute universal significance.

FROM CHURCH TO WORLD: CONTINUITY BETWEEN THE SECULAR CITY AND THE KINGDOM

Of all the needs felt by Catholics as the Council opened probably few were more felt, especially by Europeans and

---

[7]"Uniqueness" itself as predicated of Jesus is a debatable notion among Catholic theologians, cf. E. Schillebeeckx, *Jesus* (New York: Seabury, 1979); J. Mackey, *Jesus: The Man and the Myth* (New York: Paulist, 1979); P. Knitter, "World Religions and the Finality of Christ," *Horizons* 5 (1978) 151-164.

Americans, than the need for the Catholic ghetto to end and a new posture toward the world to be assumed. The response of the Council can be seen in the range of its concerns. Its constitution *Gaudium et Spes*, on the *Church in the Modern World*, wants to address all persons. Moreso than any previous Council, Vatican II took cognizance of the world around it and viewed it necessary to engage the world as conversation partner. Its pastoral concerns ran beyond the confines of Roman Catholicism, indeed beyond Christianity, to a universal, cosmic horizon. It evaluated the world positively, stated the Church's desire to service the world, acknowledged the impact of the world on the Church, and professed its intention to be a formative influence in the new era aborning. This shift in focus from the Church to the world emerged within a network of conflicting expectations and with little felt need to probe more deeply the implications of what a new posture vis-à-vis the world might concretely mean.

Yet undeniably this perhaps most novel of Vatican II's documents provides a wholly new vision of the relationship between Church and world.[8] It acknowledges the autonomy of secular culture, especially of science; it summons the Church to update its doctrines and institutions and to appropriate the best achievements of the modern world. The Church is to respect secular life and learn from it, lest it become anachronistic and impotent to herald the gospel. It affirms that the Church must see itself as part of the human family, sharing the common concerns of all men and women, who are its conversation partners.[9]

Vatican II's secularity however poses problems as yet unresolved. Was the Council mandating, however implicitly, the emergence of something truly novel in Roman Catholicism? Or was it "just the world" being looked at in a new way? But is it possible to have a new vision of one,

---

[8]*Gaudium et Spes*, n. 2. The "world" refers to "the whole human family along with the sum total of those realities in the midst of which the human family lives."

[9]*Ibid.*, n. 62.

Church or world, without at the same time seeing the other anew as well? John Paul II has challenged theologians and bishops "to carry out serious reflection on the relationship between evangelization and human advancement or liberation, taking into consideration...what is specific about the Church's presence."[10] What is the style of religiously based socio-political ministry, then, is one of the questions of a post-conciliar Church. Moreover, to link religious identity and political mission is not merely to seek a theological legitimation of the Church's involvement in social justice, but also to search for the very meaning of the Church. The Church is more than a lobby or a welfare agency. It claims a distinctive religious identity, and to be Church that identity must surface in its style of political praxis. Interestingly, the Pastoral Constitution *Gaudium et Spes* with its centrifugal thrust stresses the continuity between the secular values of human dignity, freedom, brotherhood, and earthly progress, and their consummation in the Kingdom. The world is accepted as the arena where these values struggle to become reality and hope of the kingdom animates the quest for earthly justice and peace. The imagery of fruit and flower and the optimistic language of growth and development are employed. Teilhard de Chardin's predeliction for biological and organic metaphors may be at work here.[11] In any case, the Council shied away from the hard question of the nature of the relationship between human progress and the Kingdom coming to be. It does not give its seal of approval to the Teilhardian view that building the secular city is a vital element for the future Kingdom, indeed a *condito sine qua non.* The Council is content to steer a pastoral middle course between supernaturalism and naturalism and to proclaim a believing, Christological humanism.

Many, concerned about the thorough-going optimism of *Gaudium et Spes* would ask Karl Barth's questions about

---

[10]*John Paul II in Mexico: Addresses and Homilies* (Washington, D.C.: U.S.C.C., 1979), Puebla Address, 3,1.

[11]On the Council's linguistics, see L. O'Donovan, "Was Vatican II Evolutionary? A Note on Conciliar Language," *Theological Studies* 36 (1975) 493-502.

the Constitution. Does its naive optimism about the possibility of world development find a warrant in the Pauline writings and the synoptic gospels? Is it so clear that dialogue with and service to the world is to hold primacy over proclamation to the world? Paul Tillich puts it well. He observed that the Church has in fact contributed much to Western Civilization. But "a Church that is nothing more than a benevolent, socially useful group can be replaced by other groups not claiming to be Churches: such a Church has no justification for its existence."[12]

III. The Impact of the Council: Radical Discontinuity

In an address opening the first session of the Council, October 11, 1962, John XXIII spoke of introducing into the Church "appropriate emendations."[13] In regard to doctrine, John spoke, perhaps naively, of the permissibility, even the necessity, of dressing up the old truths in new words. The conservative tone of his remarks is suggested by the fact that they seem to allude to Vatican I's Constitution on the Catholic Faith, *Dei Filius*. Moreover, the Council itself proposed a program of *ressourcement* as a safety valve. A return to the sources was to assure that in effecting pastoral accomodations to modernity, only that would be changed from the past which was truly patient of change. At each critical juncture the question of the relationship of the past to the present appears and is laid to rest with the paternal assurance that no substantial change is being made in the heritage of the past.

But the change that Vatican II set in motion was more radical perhaps than its framers ever realized. Hubert Jedin has opined that the perennial spirit of Catholic reform is epitomized by Giles of Viterbo (1469-1532), Prior General of the Augustinians, in his inaugural address at the 5th Lateran Council: "Men must be changed by religion, not religion by men." This is the classicist and primitivist view of

[12]P. Tillich, *Systematic Theology, III* (Chicago: University of Chicago, 1963) 166.

[13]*A.A.S.* 54 (1962) 788.

history, oriented to the past, with little awareness of social
change or novelty except insofar as change is for the worse,
is decline from a superior pristine condition.[14] God is the
chief agent in history and all legitimate change is his doing
alone. Changes effected by humans are sacrilegious. True
reform is the removal of human hindrances to the sacred.
Just so, people were to be changed by religion, not religion
by people. But Vatican II's challenge of accommodation to
the times called for precisely the opposite. It decreed that
religion should be changed by people, so as to meet the
needs of people. In this Vatican II stands in radical discontinuity with all the councils preceding it. Two decades later a
minimalist interpretation of Vatican II's accommodation
appears only wishful and no longer possible. In the scope
and depth of its implications *aggiornamento* was a revolution in the Catholic history of the idea of reform. It is now
impossible to restrain the thrust of *aggiornamento* within
the minimalist limits drawn by the past. The goals and
purposes, the dynamic logic of reform outstrip any limita-
tions many Council fathers may have had in mind.

Certainly Vatican II is much concerned about continuity
with the past and fidelity to it. Nonetheless, more than any
of the 20 preceding councils it recognizes that the Church
lives in a world whose historical consciousness has been
heightened.[15] The Council manifests a sensitivity to change,
to discontinuity, and indeed an Enlightenment perspective
on the movement of history which is forward looking and
expressible in the generic word "progress." As applied to the
life of the Church, growth, progress, development become
for the first time major conciliar motifs. Fidelity to the
patrimony of the past becomes developmental continuity.
Surprisingly, the area to which this generic notion of progress is most frequently applied is that of doctrine.
Obviously, the question of doctrinal development is a part
of the larger question of corporate identity. By comparison
to Vatican II's many allusions to a maturation, to progress,

[14]O'Malley, *loc. cit.*, 592 ff.

[15]W. Bassett, "Canon Law and Reform: An Agenda for a New Beginning," in
Toward Vatican III, eds. D. Tracy et al. (New York: Seabury, 1978) 198 ff.

evolution, and growing understanding of doctrine, what Vatican I cautiously has to say on the subject is sparse, though in an age taken with biological evolution and historical progress and 25 years after Newman's essay on doctrinal development, it is the first council to admit, minimally, the possibility of doctrinal development. Nevertheless, Vatican II's treatment of *how* doctrinal development occurs is indeed jejune. And there is just as much vagueness as to how the general progress of the Church takes place. The term "progress," moreover, is less frequently employed to describe what is occurring in the Church than are, with some incoherence, the traditional terms of previous councils, "renewal," "restoration," "rejuvenation" (*renovare, instaurare, inuvenescere*). What is suggested is cyclical, repetitive historical patterns more than linear progression.

A CALL TO REFORM AND DENIAL

It is striking that given the discontinuity with its predecessors, the one traditional term conspicuously absent from the Vatican II corpus is the word "reform" or "reformation." It appears only once in connection with the Church in the remarkable *Decree on Ecumenism*.[16] The decree mandates reform of ecclesial institutional life. Speaking of faults in violation of ecclesial unity, it twice acknowledges that Catholics shoulder a share of the blame. And twice it calls for reform. In the first instance "reform" is synonymous with "renovation" and appears to signify reform of individual christians. In the second instance we have in a conciliar text, for the first time since Basel (1431-1437) sounded its call for a reform in "head and members," a clarion call to "reform of the Church."

> "Christ summons the Church as she goes on her pilgrim way to that continual *reformation (ad hanc perennem reformationem)* of which she always has need, insofar as she is an institution of men here on earth. Therefore if the

[16]O'Malley, *loc. cit.,* 587.

influence of events or of the times have led to deficiencies (*quae minus accurate servata fuerint*) in moral conduct, in Church discipline, or even in the formulation of doctrine...These should be appropriately rectified at the proper moment."[17]

In this text clearly it is the Church as a people and as a social system that stands in need of *ongoing* reform. Never will conduct, discipline, and doctrine arrive at irreformable perfection. The *quae minus accurate servata fuerint* of the text is a stark contrast to Trent's evaluation of its own doctrine of the Eucharist as *omni ex parte perfecta*. And Trent in this merely makes explicit for one of its teachings a presupposition underlying all its doctrinal pronouncements. Further, the text's depiction of the Church as on pilgrimage correlates with the Council's principal image of the Church as "the people of God." Both images lay bare the old theological slight of hand which distinguished a perfect and faithful Church unblemished by stain or wrinkle from the Christian people subject to sin. This recognition of the Church's historicity opened the door to a reform of institutions and laws in the Church though the Council nowhere ratifies such a reading. But today, two decades later, Rome in its so-called revision of Church law has turned a deaf ear to the Council's call for reform and sees no need for any major structural change.[18]

While Vatican II's soft word *aggiornamento* entails hard revolutionary dimensions that can make for radical discontinuities with the past, there seems to be little evidence that the Council itself or the post conciliar church has yet taken seriously the possibility of the new opened up by modern historical consciousness. Reluctance to admit radical discontinuities in history has been and remains "a classical Catholic strategem." This strategem is rooted in a lack of a

[17]*Unitatis Redintegratio*, n. 6.

[18]R. McBrien, "A Theologian Looks at the Role of Law in the Church Today," *Proc. Canon Law Society of America*, 1981, 18-31; T. Green, "Revision of Canon Law: Theological Implications," *Theological Studies* 40 (1979) 593-679.

critical sensitivity to the allegedly authentic past as contingent, human, and culturally conditioned with the result that
it must be desacralized, relativised, and neutralized. And
just because it is so, humans are able to admit of realities and
values, even in the Church, *quae minus accurate servata
fuerint* and hence are free to imaginatively create a future.
This consciousness in fact has been at the heart of all true
reform. Failure to arrive at this type of critical consciousness removes Church structures from human examination
and renders theologians and historians superfluous. And so
the post-conciliar period has not been without its serious
tensions. Some have a new understanding of themselves as
beings of radical historicity, which imposes revolutionary
ways of thinking and acting about reform. Some, often
enough in the corridors of power, cleave to the illusion that
the past will tell us what to do. [19]

HERMENEUTICAL AMBIGUITY

This institutional crisis is due, then, to a war between two
different paradigms. It has led to polarization, mutual
incomprehension, inability to communicate, frustration,
and indifference. It is also due to the very inconsistency and
ambiguity that, perhaps inevitably, mark the Council's
teaching. The Council sent out conflicting signals. It laid
down principles which theologically justify sweeping
reforms in the structures and postures of the Church. In
essence a pilgrim people, it should be open to participatory
democratic procedures of subsidiarity and collegiality. Its
basic aim should not be the salvation of souls abstracted
from their historical and social situations, but rather the
sanctification of the world and unification of all human
kind in anticipation of the kingdom. As these revolutionary
principles were enunciated, the formulations of the past
were simultaneously rehearsed. Vatican I's teaching on
papal ultimacy was ruthlessly inserted without modification
or reinterpretation into the third chapter of the *Lumen
Gentium* where the collegiality of the episcopacy is pres-

[19]O'Malley, *loc. cit.,* 579 ff.

ented and a radically different vision of the church. Similarly, individualistic, eschatological other worldliness lies side by side with a cosmic, social eschatology which renders the humanization of cultural and social structures a primary Christian duty.[20]

There is something here for everyone. Progressives and traditionalists, biblicists and ultramontanes can all appeal to aspects of conciliar teaching and find in them the hermeneutic key to an exegesis of the whole. To a large extent the ambiguity was deliberate and necessary. To win as broad a consensus as possible and to reflect the full scope of Catholic belief old and new were juxtaposed, leaving it an open question whether the new is interpreted in light of the old or vice versa. Many thought of this as purely political compromise, of no practical import, but giving the hierarchy broader freedom in interpreting and implementing the conciliar decrees, with the Catholic people and its ministers docile and obedient. As it turned out, the rank and file in many cases gave their obedience not to Church leaders but to what they took to be even more authoritative, the Council documents.[21] Nevertheless the hierarchy has retained tremendous power, controlling as they do, and with little accountability, purse and policy, appointments and information flow. For Vatican II never translated its decentralizing emphases into Church institutions. Statements about collegiality and lay responsibility ring hollow when not structurally assured. For some this is the failure of Vatican II; for others it is too soon to expect dramatic structural reform in this regard. But meanwhile power is perceived as misused when bishops transgress what many in the Church consider to be the import of the Council documents. The conflict of interpretations and ecclesiologies, however, in both professional and popular circles, is not rooted merely in differing exegesis of inconsistent texts. The roots are also

[20]G. Lindbeck, "The Crisis in American Catholicism," in *Our Common History as Christians*, ed. J. Deschner et al. (New York: Oxford, 1975) 47-66.

[21]C. F. Oakley, "The 'New Conciliarism' and Its Implications: A Problem in History and Hermeneutics," *Journal of Ecumenical Studies* 8 (1971) 815-840.

differing attitudes regarding social movements such as
Marxism, regarding modern philosophical developments,
regarding the theology of Providence and the *jus divinum* as
they concern elements of Christianity, and, as we saw, differing attitudes regarding the delicate balance between continuity and discontinuity in the process of change. In a
word, there is a conflict of horizons.

This ambiguity and the spectrum of interpretations that
has ensued cannot easily be dissolved. It must be lived
through. As Constantinople quelled the tempest raised by
Nicea, and Chalcedon by Ephesus, settlement may come
only through another Council, which should not be rushed.
For time is needed to allow a new consensus and a new
Catholicism to emerge, one which sees its destiny inseparable from the issue of Christian unity and realizes the full
ecumenicity of any council demands participation by all
Christian communions.

THE DIALECTIC BETWEEN PAST AND PRESENT

When all is said and done, the problem arising from the
new Pentecost the Council fathers experienced and the
aggiornamento they mandated is a fundamental one: the
relationship of the past to the present. *Aggiornamento* was
not born of an understanding of that relationship which was
common to all the fathers. Nor did the Council mandate its
changes for a Church which enjoyed any such common
understanding. The results have been cataclysmic. Roman
Catholicism is not merely going through a phase of self
correction, of revival, or of adaptation to modernity. It is
slowly transmuting even while clinging to the soft word
aggiornamento. Where reform is the order of the day, the
dialectic between continuity and discontinuity is decisive.
Lacking a shared understanding of it, the Council's summons to accommodate while holding to the authentic past
became less a practical norm than an explosive problematic.
The answer to such a problematic is in function of what one
thinks the Church should be.[22]

[22]O'Malley, *loc. cit.*, 589ff.

The fall out has been visible to all — the decline in Mass attendance, the virtual demise of the Sacrament of Reconciliation (entailing the clergy's diminished social control), selective obedience to the magisterium, an upswing in divorce, a quantitative and qualitative downswing in religious and priestly vocations, the vertiginous confusion of theological pluralism, an often mindless capitulation to *modernitas*, the malaise of those for whom Catholicism as a stable world of meaning has shattered, and with it the faith that cultural system mediated and sustained with its web of symbols. That world, gone now, for many, gave visible historical continuity, assured one he was in the ark of salvation, drew a clean line between friends and foes of the faith. It was a world of pilgrimages, conclaves, incense, lace albs, novenas, monsignors, papal knights, bulding drives, and above all, clear rules to govern all aspects of life. Its requiem has been decried in the work of James Hitchcock, chronicled by Gary Wills, and, more recently dramatized in the novels of Mary Gordon. Sadly enough, many have yet to achieve a second naiveté about Catholicism as a religious symbol system. Some bitterly, some wistfully share Simone Weil's sentiment that "the loss of the past, collective or individual, is the great human tragedy, and we have thrown ours away as a child tears up a rose." Many have borne a pain largely unattended by "new Catholics" who have no roots in the tradition.

Soon after the Council counter trends established themselves in the Roman Curia, in some episcopal conferences, and among many lay Catholics. In a first step they interpreted Council texts in the light of their more traditional passages. More recently they have tried with some success to subtly checkmate the Council by benign neglect, regressive guidelines for implementation, and finally by a code of law which in many ways ignores the ecclesial vision of Vatican II. These retrogressive tactics caused many whose hearts were set on reform to lose confidence and to move to the periphery of the Church where they maintain a posture of indifference to and minimal participation in the life of the larger community. Still others resorted to wild, uncontrolled reform initiatives which triggered further hierarchical backlash so that even more reform-minded bishops called for retreat. The Lefebvre movement to save the Church by annulling the Council is only a more blatant example of post-conciliar loss of nerve. Of course, there were yet others who, unable to cope with post-conciliar change, polarization, and uncertainty, sought relief in a "retreat to commitment" and the false security of shallow pietism.

IV. Pressing Agenda

ECUMENISM: NEW ECCLESIOLOGICAL MODELS

The progress of bilateral and multilateral ecumenical discussion over the past fourteen years has reached a critical stage. The neuralgic point has shifted from theoretical theological questions to practical issues of polity. Many feel that the decisive classical controversial issues have reached substantial resolution and the remaining differences are no longer divisive. Thus there is a growing desire that church authorities take the steps necessary to bring informal contact and theological dialogue to term in some form of reciprocal recognition and unification. Lacking that, increased irenicism appears to be meaningless acceleration while idling. Slowness to move forward stems in part from Rome's mistrust of conceptual theological agreements on the first three articles of the creed and its focus on the fourth article, the church in its concrete shape, its putative apostolic polity and sacramental practice. On a deeper level, this is a manifestation of the Catholic ethos which views incarnationalism and sacramentalism as elements of authentic conversion and therefore mistrusts protestant "spiritualism," the privatization of religion, and any orthodoxy that is too hieratic and withdrawn, all of which, by the way, is often detectable in the "Protestant" Catholics who are our students.

The first need, therefore, is to protect the principles of

Unitatis Redintegratio against the retrenchment and obfuscation of recent years lest they die the death of a thousand qualifications. Endangered by a lack of understanding and ecumenical commitment, the half dozen basic principles needing emphasis are these. The Church of Christ is not exclusively identical with the Roman Catholic Church, but is also present in other christian communities. Secondly, sharing the reality of the one church, these communities already share with each other a real though imperfect union. Thirdly, this real but partial communion necessarily calls for articulation in common witness, worship, and service. Fourthly, the residual differences which stand in the way of full unity are important and each group must cling to its integrity and its conviction against any false unity. Next, the finality of ecumenism is not for the churches to return home to Rome, which sits back waiting its play with the calm confidence of a christian holding four aces, but for all to converge in the gospel, there to find full ecclesial union. Finally, serious dialogue must be ongoing. Here are six clear points not widely understood and internalized by Catholic clergy and laity.[23] They have been, like Musak, heard but not heard.

In the post-conciliar years the lines that have separated the Christian churches have become very fluid. Conservative Catholics and Lutherans resemble one another and the real division lies between them and their progressive counterparts in the Lutheran and Catholic camps. Less and less do theologians disagree along confessional lines but more and more on academic grounds. Those whom creeds put asunder critical method has united. Dialogue has replaced polemic. Theologians are now so deep inside each other's skin that no offense is taken when the "outsider" questions the cornerstone of a fraternal kingdom. Given, then, clear convergence on the eucharist, on Church office, on authority the question becomes: what range of diversity is compatible with unity? Can there be unity without annihilating

---

[23]A. Dulles, "Ecumenism: Problems and Opportunities for the Future," in D. Tracy, et al., eds. *Toward Vatican III*, 91-93.

absorption? Short of full juridical union can we not have recourse to the intermediate device of a formal covenant consisting in an acknowledgement that Catholicism and the other Christian Churches are intermediate, penultimate forms of the one Church in process; a public recognition of ministries, and an extension of Eucharistic hospitality in some cases, and finally a pact to collaborate in social action?[24]

Vatican II implicitly disassociated itself from the model of full juridical union under an immutable Rome (a single organized church, with one government and the same doctrines and sacraments), which was the goal of early Catholic ecumenism.[25] It did so by linking reunion to reform, by acknowledging deficiencies in Roman Catholicism, and by urging other Christian communities not to abandon what in them is the work of the Spirit.[26] The *una sancta* is a joint venture, fulfilling but mutating all the churches that enter it.

Nevertheless, a lingering presupposition behind much post-conciliar thinking about reunion is the notion that communion is more perfect to the extent that differences are purged. Christ is thought to have endowed his church with a patrimony channeled through the apostles. Christian unity therefore is contingent upon a shared acceptance of that patrimony. Perhaps this ecclesiology of substance and preservation should yield to one of process and response better suited to innovation and pluralism. Why cannot the churches provide an indeterminate variety of improvisations on the christian theme, all of which would refract in their own time and place something of the richness of the gospel? Unity would not signify uniform clinging to a supposed apostolic patrimony, but rather the dynamic interaction of a network of autonomous denominations. If ecumenism is not to lie dead in the water this model, best suited today, should be pursued, not an agreement to disagree, but a covenanted heterogenous community of mutual

---

[24]On models of union cf. *Ibid.*, 93-99.

[25]Cf. Pius XI, *Mortalium Animos*, 1928.

[26]*Unitatis Redintegratio*, ns. 4 and 6.

witness, dialogue, shared action, and in some instances shared cult.

Since the Council ecumenically-sensitive theologians have capitalized on what concessions the Council made to a non-substantialist ecclesiology instead of fixating on the substantialist elements in the council corpus. Goaded by the critical probing of scholarship, Catholics are more aware than ever of the difficulty of differentiating between essentials and accidentals in the life of christianity. The institutional and the pneumatic are in tension and the former is subordinated to the mission of the Church. A dramatic change has occurred in that the *onus probandi* now rests with those who wish to maintain that a given element is *jure divino* immutable.[27] The drift is toward accenting what believers share in common, not what separates them. In a word, an idealist ecclesial model is in vogue, the vision of a Church patterned after the unfolding of the self.[28] Because of the radical temporality of revelation and faith, there is no ideal Church. It can be found only at the end of the eschatological process. The Church is forever and necessarily becoming the Christian community, for it is an unfinished essence, processing from potency to act, incarnationally realizing the Spirit. It is a collective transcendental self, in this idealist post-conciliar ecclesiology, knowing many stages as the community realizes its essence in historical forms which serve as symbolic embodiment of the Spirit of God. Thus the Church's nature is not fully given at the start, nor fully realized or displayed in any one epoch. It is unfolding. This organic, evolving, idealist ecclesiological model tends to relativize past and present ecclesial bodies which together form the one Church.

The fragmenting of Christianity into an array of competing churches, on the other hand, weakens christian witness in the world and betrays the values it proclaims. It impedes

---

[27]On *jus divinum* cf. A. Dulles, *A Church to Believe In* (New York: Crossroad, 1983), c. 6.

[28]T. O'Meara, "Philosophical Models in Ecclesiology," *Theological Studies* 29 (1978) 3-21.

secular society, racked by divisions of its own, from turning to the churches for healing. And the dream of the *una sancta* loses its lure. For "any presumption of an eternal metaphysical definition for the church undermines its historical and eschatological nature. It belongs to the essence of the church to change. The forms of cultural history are the lessons of ecclesiology."[29]

The other reigning post-conciliar ecclesiological model is phenomenological. It too refuses to deduce a formal structure from a perfect definition of an essence of the Church. Rather it begins with a cluster of forms seeing there an emerging but only partially disclosed nature. Disclosure occurs in history with the forms of cultural history as the bridges by which reality reaches our perception. Yet with every revealment goes concealment. Full reality is never apprehended. As an historical entity the church is grasped through the forms of a particular time. This model passes over the evolutionary stance of the idealist model wherein through history the church tends to a fuller and better disclosure. Each epoch can disclose her life. Essence and form are inseparable. There is no chemically pure essence distilled from the stream of historical forms. Thus rather than lamenting the pluralistic diversity of Christianity, ecclesiology should rejoice in it. No single ecclesiology is *the* correct one. The full nature of the Church eludes paradigm. We glimpse the real church only if we see it existing in its varying historical forms and colors rather than existing above and beyond them.[30]

RELIGIOUS IDENTITY AND SOCIO-POLITICAL INVOLVEMENT

While the Council began opening the Church to the world in the early 60's amid a time of great optimism, the society of the 70's and 80's grows disillusioned to the point of cultural pessimism. Ecology, the world economy, nuclear power,

---

[29]*Ibid.*, 21.

[30]H. Küng, *The Church* (New York: Sheed & Ward, 1967) 5f.

and demography charge at us, four deadly horsemen threatening the rebarbarization of our fragile civilization.[31] Thus the Council's showpiece *Gaudium et Spes* appears somewhat naive twenty years later in a world that now is obviously both promise and menace.

Moreover an epochal new situation has emerged and a challenge of the first order confronts Catholicism. The world's problems can no longer be viewed purely in terms of an East-West conflict. Important as that conflict is, it is, perhaps, being superseded by a North-South conflict, by a conflict between the rich North Atlantic nations and the poverty-stricken areas of the South, which traditionally have been peopled by Catholics. One estimate is that by the year 2000 70% of all Catholics will be found in the 3rd world. How does a European and North American Catholicism come to terms with this conflict along the North-South axis if it encompasses both in itself? The answer will determine whether Catholicism becomes *de facto* and for the first time a world Church or remains a europocentric Church with colonies in the poor areas of the world.[32]

Even though the Church becomes political simply by proclaiming the dignity of the personhood and existence of all men and women as subjects before God, it must come down on the side of this dignity in those areas where it is endangered. The Church must struggle not only so that humans *remain* subjects under the pressures of industrialism and totalitarianism, but also that they *become* subjects by transcending misery and oppression. This means postconciliar ecclesial problems of identity and social legitimation cannot be solved in a purely hermeneutical way but only by a praxis that is discipleship with its mystical-political dialectic, which has been the basis of recent political Christologies. These in turn attempt to ground a move

[31] R. Heilbroner, *An Inquiry into the Human Prospect* 2 ed. (New York: W. W. Norton, 1980).

[32] P. Nichols, *The Pope's Divisions* (New York: Holt, Rhinehart, Winston, 1982); K. Rahner, "Toward a Fundamental Theological Interpretation of Vatican II," *Theological Studies* 40 (1979) 716-727.

from a populist-traditional Church-for-the-people to a Church of solidarity, a Church-of-the-people.

All this raises the thorny issue of the link between socio-political activity and Catholicism's religious identity, an issue which has come to the fore in the post-conciliar era due to the burgeoning of political and liberation theology.[33] The Church fails to be church if such a ministry is not an expression of its religious identity. Neo-scholasticism, which drove a wedge between the natural and the supernatural, viewed any social or political activities as an inauthentic ministry. Even *Gaudium et Spes* states that Christ gave the Church "no proper mission in the political, economic, or social order. The purpose which he set before her is a religious one."[34] In this view the Church's primary task is evangelization not civilization. Immanent concerns must not edge out the transcendent. Obviously, an overly facile nature-grace dualism undergirds this position. In reaction, a second position views the socio-political activities of the Church as temporary, subsidiary, substitutive for the deficiencies of personnel and institutions in secular agencies.[35] The Church should formally and institutionally engage itself in a social mission only where secular agencies do not attend to imperative needs. This view, again, dichotomizes religious and secular and views a social mission as improper except in exceptional circumstances. How can it explain the history of Catholicism in which a social mission has appeared at all times integral to the Church's mission?

[33]For what follows I am indebted to the work of F. Fiorenza. Cf. "Political Theology and Liberation Theology: An Inquiry into their Fundamental Meaning," in *Liberation, Freedom, and Revolution*, ed. T. McFadden (New York: Seabury, 1975) 3-29. "Political Theology as Foundational Theology," *Proc. C.T.S.A.* 32 (1977); "The Church's Religious Identity and Its Social and Political Mission," *Theological Studies* 43 (1982) 197-225.

[34]*Gaudium et Spes*, n. 42.

[35]W. Pannenberg, *Theology and the Kingdom of God* (Philadelphia: Westminster, 1969) 90-91; R. McBrien, "The Church and Social Change: An Ecclesiological Critique," in *Theology Confronts a Changing World*, ed. T. McFadden (West Mystic: Twenty Third, 1977) 41-62; J. Segundo, *The Community Called Church* (Maryknoll: Orbis, 1972) 96. Note that in *Catholicism II* (Minneapolis: Winston, 1980) 720-722 McBrien adopts a more constitutive position.

A third position argues for an unofficial social mission. "The Church *as an official* Church is not the immediate or proper subject for realizing the concrete humanization of the world."[36] The Church is unqualified to do so and the right and responsibility to do so belong to the secular sphere. Any other proposal amounts to a subtle reintroduction of clericalism and integralism. The Church may motivate and inspire groups of lay christians to unofficial and voluntary service of the world. With this position new dichotomies are introduced: official religious mission/unofficial social mission; hierarchical, ecclesial/lay, secular. Priests engaged in secular tasks do what is properly lay activity. Laity engaged in religious work should somehow be clericalized, ordained, e.g., the diaconate.

A fourth and more analytical position sees pluriformity in Church models and tasks. Because service is one ecclesial task, social and political action are integral to the life of the Church. Of great concern to this position is the preservation of the Church's distinctive mission and identity as they strive to articulate themselves in social action.[37] Some would claim the sacramental and kerygmatic functions of the Church are primary while the servant function is essential but secondary, though not improper or unofficial. The difficulty with this analytical perspective is its risk of fragmenting the Church's activities into disconnected compartments. Further, post-conciliar liberation and political theology have appealed to eschatology to link evangelization and socio-political activities. Political theology has stressed the socio-political implications of the Church's proclamation of the kingdom. This eschatological vision, however, orients the Church's political mission primarily if not exclusively to negative criticism of oppressive ideologies and institutions. It offers no recipe of reform, no specific

---

[36]K. Rahner, "The Church's Commission to bring Salvation and the Humanization of the World," *Theological Investigations* XIV (New York: Seabury) 295-313.

[37]A. Dulles, "The Meaning of Faith Considered in Relationship to Justice," in *The Faith That Does Justice*, ed. J. Haughey (New York: Paulist, 1977) 1-46.

political remedies.[38] Some liberation theologians, on the other hand, stressing the unity of salvation history and world history and linking eschatology and liberation, envision the Church as more than negative critic. The Church positively struggles to make real in history partial but genuine anticipations of the kingdom. Here there is an emphasis on human development as the kingdom aborning. The danger in this, according to the critics, is a reductionism that collapses the christian message into social and political ideology and the Church into a reform movement.

In the post-conciliar period the magisterium has tried to balance and nuance the distinction between the Church's evangelizing and civilizing activities without collapsing one into the other. In 1971 the International Synod of Bishops stated: "Action on behalf of justice and participation in the transformation of the world appear to us a constitutive dimension of the preaching of the gospel... of the Church's mission for the redemption of the human race and its liberation from every oppressive situation."[39] The key word is "constitutive." Social Action is not improper or secondary, but constitutive of evangelization. The International Theological Commission interprets "constitutive" to mean "integral," not "essential."[40] But the Commission does assert that if transformation of the world is lacking, a distortion of the christian message occurs.

In 1974 Paul VI challenged the Third Assembly of the Synod of Bishops to define the relationship between evangelization and human development: "It will be necessary to define more accurately the relationship between evangelization... and the human effort toward development for which the Church's help is rightly expected, though this is not her specific task."[41] The Synod responded with two documents,

[38] J. B. Metz, *Faith in History and Society* (New York: Seabury, 1980); J. Hehir, "The Idea of a Political Theology," *Worldview* 14 (1971) 5-7.

[39] "De Justitia in Mundo" in *The Gospel of Peace and Justice,* ed. J. Gremillon (Maryknoll: Orbis, 1976) 513-529 at 514.

[40] *Human Development and Christian Salvation* in *Origins* 7 (Nov. 1977) 311.

[41] *Catholic Mind* 73 (1975) 6.

one stating that "the promotion of human rights is required by the gospel and central to her ministry,"[42] the other affirming an "intimate connection between evangelization and liberation."[43] This second document maintains that while evangelization and liberation are interrelated, salvation is more than the present liberation the Church now begins to effect. Subsequently, in his *Evangelization in The Modern World*, Paul VI dialectically relates and distinguishes evangelization and human liberation. The two are related because the Church's mission is to relate the gospel to human social life and because links exist between them on the level of anthropology, theology, and the gospel. Anthropology: The subject evangelized is concretely situated amid social and political structures.[44] Theology: *all* creation yearns for redemption. The Gospel: love of neighbor includes the proclamation of justice and peace.[45] Yet the two are distinct, for some forms of liberation are incompatible with the gospel and evangelization encompasses more than socio-political liberation since it touches human sinfulness, the root of injustice.[46] Distinct though they are, each is incomplete without the other. Evangelization has the primacy, but includes, transforms, and extends beyond liberation. Salvation embraces liberation from all that oppresses persons, especially sin.[47]

Though John Paul II's writings are not wholly free of ambiguity, the same dialectic marks his Puebla address and his letters *Redemptor hominis* and *Laborem exercens*. According to John Paul "Evangelization is the essential

[42] *Ibid.*, 50-51.

[43] *Ibid.*, 55.

[44] John Paul advances Paul VI's anthropological nexus of Evangelization and liberation by an appeal to Christology. Evangelization is concerned with concrete persons in specific social systems, but beneath all systemic violence is an inauthentic image of humanity. Against it the Church sets an image of personhood derived from Christology.

[45] *Evangelii nuntiandi* (Wash. D.C.: U.S.C.C., 1976) n. 31.

[46] *Ibid.*, nos. 34-35.

[47] *Ibid.*, n. 9.

mission...the deepest identity of the Church" but action for social justice is also constitutive of the Church's mission. The Church's mission he states, is "religious and not political or social" but this religious mission must impact all facets of social life.[48] In a word, John Paul does relate earthly development to the growth of the kingdom.

From this survey Fiorenza derives two conclusions.[49] The magisterium affirms dedication to social justice integral to the Church's mission and is struggling with the dialectical relationship between religious identity and social mission. Post-conciliar documents ground the relationship in the dignity of the person and the love command. Eschatology, however, indicates that Evangelization cannot be wholly and exclusively identified with earthly progress and liberation. Thus a note of discontinuity is struck and a contrast to recent political and liberation theologies. The former appeals to eschatology to justify a critical political function for the Church. The latter views eschatological salvation as the perfection of human liberation and argues the two are intrinsically linked. Hence the post-conciliar magisterium adheres more closely to *Lumen Gentium* than to *Gaudium et Spes* on the role of eschatology. *Lumen Gentium* stresses the Eschaton as goal; *Gaudium et Spes* as a light for focusing the Church's vocation in the world.

Conciliar and post-conciliar documents, therefore, point to an unresolved issue: to ascertain how the struggle for justice properly pertains to the work of the Church and to determine the style of a social and political ministry. More is involved here than merely a religious justification of the Church's social involvement. The very identity of the Church is at stake. The function and identity of religion are uncovered only by attending to the self-reflection and praxis of the religion itself. Ecclesial identity cannot be defined in isolation from the other dimensions of life but only in its interaction with them. The search for self understanding as

[48]Puebla Address, 1,7 and 3,2.
[49]"Church's Religious Identity," *loc. cit.*, 209-210.

it evolves through praxis is part of Catholicism's pressing agenda as it cautiously moves toward the end of a century that has opened it to radical change.

VATICAN II AND THE AMERICAN EXPERIENCE OF CHURCH

Avery Dulles, S.J.

My topic is an extremely broad one, and I shall be able to treat it only in a hasty, impressionistic way. My intention will be to point out that the participation of Americans at Vatican Council II, and the interpretation and impact of the council in this country, were conditioned, in part, by the peculiar characteristics of American Catholicism in the middle of the twentieth century. I shall contend that, while the American experience has made, and should make, a significant difference for our current understanding of Catholicism, the Catholic tradition has a reciprocal contribution to make, enriching the American experience of Church. The American dream, therefore, should not be our principal norm for interpreting or assessing Vatican II.

My presentation will be divided into three main sections: first, the American experience of Church in the decades preceding Vatican II; second, work of the council; third, the interpretation and impact of the council in the United States.

As I begin I am conscious of a problem of language. My title contains the word, "American." While this word could be interpreted to mean all countries in North and South America, I shall understand it as referring simply to the United States. Unfortunately we do not have in English any adjective specifically designating what pertains to the United States of America, so we use the term "American." I hope our Canadian and other non-United Statesers will bear with this usage.

1. The American Catholic Experience Before the Council

Since the seventeenth century American Catholics have had many experiences of Church, most of which were only faint memories by the end of World War I. With the condemnation of the so-called Americanist heresy by Pope Leo XIII in 1899 and the rejection of Modernism by Pius X in 1907, many earlier trends were simply crushed. The large Catholic immigrations from Western Europe in the latter half of the nineteenth century and the early years of the twentieth, together with the influx of European priests and religious, brought about, by 1920, an era in American Catholicism that was somewhat discontinuous with the preceding history. In the period between the first and second world wars, certain common features became characteristic of the Catholic Church in this country. These features correspond to my own experience of Catholicism, when I first came into contact with it in New York and New England during the 1930s. The Catholicism of this period has recently been described in recent works by William Halsey[1] and James Hennesey.[2]

Relying on my own impressions, as well as sources such as these, I would venture to characterize the Catholicism of the 1930's somewhat as follows. First, the Church in this country was, as I have said, predominantly immigrant and ethnic. Apart for a few areas such as Louisiana and Southern Maryland, it did not include, unless by way of exception, the

---

[1]W. M. Halsey, *The Survival of American Innocence: Catholicism in an Era of Disillusionment (1920-1940)*. Notre Dame: Univ. of Notre Dame, 1980.

[2]James Hennesey, *American Catholics: A History of the Roman Catholic Community in the United States*. New York: Oxford Univ. Press, 1981.

established American families, but rather was made up of minorities who vividly remembered the "old country" from which they hailed.

The Catholic population, having come in many cases to escape persecution or oppression, were appreciative of their new environment, with the freedom and opportunity it offered. They tended to be patriotic and were proud of their participation in the various wars of their adopted country. But at the same time, they were not fully at home, since they still suffered from prejudice, social discrimination, and economic exploitation. They clustered together defensively in ghettos that were simultaneously religious and ethnic. The large urban ghettos provided avenues to prosperity, power, and success in certain callings. Because of the important position of the pastor, as teacher, guide, and defender of the flock, the clergy enjoyed great power and prestige. This in itself assured an abundance of vocations to the priestly and religious life. In some major cities, such as New York, Boston, and Chicago, Catholics played a prominent role in politics.

Within the relative isolation of their own communities, Catholics were well provided for, partly through the efforts of their Church. Summarizing this religious situation, Andrew Greeley has recently written:

> The rigid, often oversimplified, unquestioningly self-confident Catholicism of the first half of the present century was the result of an effort to provide poor and frequently uneducated immigrants with a simple and serviceable response to the trauma of adjusting to an unfriendly — and frequently anti-Catholic — host society.[3]

The American Catholic community of those days was not conspicuous for its intellectual and cultural life. Its cultural features were borrowed for the most part from the Catholic

[3]A. M. Greeley, "American Catholics: Going Their Own Way," *New York Times Magazine* (Oct. 10, 1982), p. 68.

countries of Western Europe. With the encouragement of Rome, American Catholics tended to look upon the Middle Ages as the golden age of faith. The title of James J. Walsh's popular book, *The Thirteenth: The Greatest of Centuries* (1907), summarized the prevalent mood. French neo-Thomists such as Jacques Maritain and Etienne Gilson, both of whom lectured frequently at American secular universities, gave respectability to medievalism in philosophy.

During the 1930s and 1940s there was a steady flow of Protestant converts into the Catholic Church. They were attracted by the cohesiveness and self-confidence of the Catholic community, by its manifest faith, and by the antiquity of its roots. Intellectuals who felt that the modern world had lost its way, and that Protestantism had excessively diluted the Christian message, turned to Catholicism for a stronger witness. The temper of such converts was reflected in the titles of their books; for example, John L. Stoddard's *Rebuilding a Lost Faith* and Ross Hoffman's *Restoration.*

Although politically most Catholics were Democrats, and suspicious of big business, they were in no sense radicals. They were nervous about the dangers of socialism and communism, but their Italian, German, and Irish extraction made them sometimes less alert to the dangers of fascism and Nazism. Halsey catches this point when he writes:

> An outbreak of 'minority-itis,' in [George N.] Shuster's view, gripped Catholics following Al Smith's defeat in 1928, the Mexican Revolution, and Catholic fears of the rising influence of Communism. In the 1930's Catholics were susceptible to the irrational appeals of anti-Semites, pro-Nazis, and Fascists.[4]

Religiously speaking, the Church stood for centralized

---

[4]*Survival of American Innocence*, p. 98. In his article, "A Catholic Defends His Church" (*New Republic* 97 [Jan. 4, 1939]), Shuster described this minority-itis as a disease consisting in "Catholic resentment against deeply ingrained non-Catholic instinct." He expressed the fear that "our democracy is breaking up into self-conscious mutually antagonistic minorities."

authority, tradition, and discipline. Catholics did not pub-
licly, or even in most cases privately, question the decisions
of their popes, bishops, and pastors. For them, the priest
stood in the place of Christ. There was a sharp line of
demarcation between clergy and laity. The liturgy reflected
this distinction of roles. The priest was set off by the communion rail; only his consecrated hands were allowed to
touch the sacred vessels as he offered sacrifice for the people
in a language understood by himself and God. There was
majesty and beauty in this liturgy, almost unchanged since
the sixteenth century, and embodying the spirituality and
art-forms of the medieval West. The Catholics of this nation
showed no disposition to introduce into their religious life
the characteristically American themes of democratization,
pluralism, experimentation, and progress. To Catholic ears,
any suggestion of this kind would have seemed close to
blasphemy.

And yet, what I have said does not represent the whole
story. A small segment of the American Catholic community were quite at home with the dominant culture of the land,
moved easily among the cultured elite, and felt that the
Church should relate more positively to the American political and intellectual tradition. George N. Shuster and many
of the contributors to *Commonweal* exemplify this tendency. In the 1940's and 50's John Courtney Murray
became the chief exponent of the thesis that there was a
natural affinity between the perennial Catholic tradition
and the American civil tradition. With some exaggeration
he wrote in his most influential book, *We Hold These
Truths*:

> Catholic participation in the American consensus has
> been full and free, unreserved and unembarassed,
> because the contents of this consensus — the ethical and
> political principles drawn from the tradition of natural
> law — approve themselves to the Catholic intelligence
> and conscience.[5]

[5]J. C. Murray, *We Hold These Truths* (New York: Sheed & Ward, 1960), p. 41.

Pursuing this line of thought, Murray contended that Catholics were closer than other Americans to the original American consensus, for they still professed the principles that had inspired the founders of the Republic, while other Americans were drifting away from the natural law tradition. Even the American principle of separation of Church and State, according to Murray, was acceptable from the Catholic point of view, for it gave Catholics the freedom to exercise their religious mission without burdening them with a legally privileged status, which had proved an incubus in many European countries.[6] The Catholic Church, Murray seemed to be saying, could do much to sustain authentic Americanism and conversely, authentic Americanism could make a valuable contribution to world Catholicism.

During the 1950's, the Murray thesis was rejected as all but heretical by some watchdogs of orthodoxy, especially at The Catholic University of America. Rome itself frowned on Murray's writings and for a time restricted his freedom to publish in his field of specialization. But Murray had a wide and enthusiastic following among younger intellectual Catholics, both clerical and lay. This was so because the kind of ghetto Catholicism I have been describing was beginning to break down. Already in World War II the majority of young, American, male Catholics were torn out of their ethnic ghettos and thrown into the American melting pot, where they survived quite well. After the war, colleges and graduate schools became for the first time open to Catholics on a large scale, thanks to new programs of government aid. The high mobility of American business and industry in the post-War period affected Catholics as much as other Americans.

Inevitably, the time soon came when Catholics were eligible for the highest positions in government and in the professions. In a dramatic reversal of the defeat of Al Smith, John F. Kennedy was elected to the presidency in 1960, and his election symbolized the emergence of Catholics to full

[6]Ibid., p. 76.

equality with Protestants in the American establishment. Speaking during the summer before the election, Gustave Weigel expressed what many felt: "The world is new. The situation of 1960 is revolutionary. It is quite unlike the world of 1900. Consequently, the relationship of the action of the laity and hierarchy must be seen in the light of the new world. We are living in a revolutionary moment."[7]

It was new, indeed, for the Catholic laity no longer to be dependent on their pastors for education, direction, and patronage. Now that they were fully accepted, they could dismantle their ideological barricades. This new situation, to be sure, gave rise to new problems. Since virtually all walks of life were now open to them, Catholics were less motivated to support specifically Catholic institutions, such as schools, hospitals, and charities. These institutions, no longer strictly needed to take care of the Catholic community, had to face questions about their continued reason for existence. There was widespread questioning in the Church, and the authoritative answers of the clergy were no longer automatically accepted.

In these changed circumstances the defensive, reactionary posture ceased to be appropriate. Catholics felt called upon to make a positive contribution to American life, and for this they were, as a group, ill prepared. Thomistic medievalism did not provide ready answers to the majority of present-day American problems. For the first time, Catholics began to take a positive interest in modern thought and in the American tradition, with the expectation of finding not only errors to refute but lessons to be learned. Some of the younger Catholics were dissatisfied with, and even perhaps ashamed of, the conservatism and parochialism of their church.

The weakening confidence in the Catholic tradition and the declining authority of priests and religious made it inevitable that soon there would be a shortage of clerical and religious vocations. Talented young men and women found that other walks of life would offer them wider oppor-

[7]Quoted by Hennesey, *American Catholics*, p. 307.

tunities for the exercise of their talents. The decline of vocations, however, was not immediate. It was partly offset by the religious boom of the 1950's.

In the 1960's there came to maturity a new generation who remembered nothing of the ghetto Catholicism of their parents — a generation educated often, at least partly, in secular institutions, articulate, financially secure, and bent upon breaking down the last barriers that excluded them from the privileges enjoyed by scions of the first families who had graduated from the name-schools of the Northeast. These young Catholics were conscious of themselves as a new breed. Their outlook was expressed by Michael Novak, who wrote in 1964 a volume entitled, *A New Generation: American and Catholic*, and also by Daniel Callahan, who published in 1965 a symposium of autobiographical essays by his contemporaries under the title *The Generation of the Third Eye*. Callahan's title was taken from an article by John Courtney Murray, under whom he had studied at Yale, and who regarded these young Catholic intellectuals as rootless, uncertain, and introspective. As Callahan's book illustrates, this generation was proudly confident of the American experiment, oriented toward experience and pragmatic results; it was rebellious against the repressive structures of the Church and the authoritarian style of parish life and preaching. It sought spiritual and intellectual nourishment from other fonts. Novak's and Callahan's books were published while Vatican II was in session, but their ideas were on the whole independent of the Council. They prove, if proof were needed, that American Catholicism was on the verge of a crisis even before Vatican II began.

2. Vatican II

The preconciliar experience of Catholics in the United States was to some extent paralleled in other countries. Since Gregory XVI and Pius IX had set their faces sternly against the liberalism of their day, Roman Catholicism had projected an image of medievalism and reaction. In France and Germany, Belgium and Holland, and to some degree in other countries, increasing numbers of intellectuals felt that the Church was paying too heavy a price for continuity with its own past. Having in effect opted out of modern culture, it was in danger of becoming intellectually, culturally, and institutionally obsolete. When Pope John XXIII called for a more positive attitude toward the modern world, the advocates of modernization, who had been under a shadow under Pius XII, began to appear as leaders. At the council, the bishops of Northern Europe, with their avant-garde theologians, arrayed themselves against what they had experienced as Roman repression and reaction.

The council proved to be a difficult struggle between the forces of the right and the left, between conservatism and progressivism. Reacting against the centralism and authoritarianism of Pius XII, many of the bishops pressed for more freedom and autonomy. For a variety of reasons, the hierarchies of the third world tended to side with the European liberals. After some initial hesitation, the American bishops gravitated toward the progressive majority, at least if their speeches and voting are a reliable index of their thinking.

A surprising thing therefore happened. The very theologians who had been under suspicion as dangerous liberals came into favor and influence. In the United States this meant that advocates of Americanization, such as John Courtney Murray and Gustave Weigel, were allied with the hierarchy against Romanizing theologians such as J. C. Fenton and Francis J. Connell. Thanks to the council, the concerns of the Americanizers became in some measure official Catholic teaching. Michael Novak went so far as to write in 1965, "The Council has made the underground official."[8]

It will not be possible here to examine this development in detail. Some summary impressions must suffice. A prime

[8]M. Novak, "American Catholicism After the Council," reprinted in his *A Time to Build* (New York: Macmillan, 1967), p. 124.

instance, of course, is the Declaration on Religious Freedom, which was, more than any other document, the special American contribution to the council. This document formally abandoned the earlier Roman position that the secular State is in principle bound to profess the Catholic faith, and admitted the concept of a religiously neutral State. Thus it accepted, in effect, the American principle of separation of Church and State. The Declaration also asserted that people must be free to inquire about matters of religion, that no one's conscience should be forced in matters of faith, and that in human society "freedom should be respected as far as possible, and curtailed only when and insofar as necessary."[9]

A second theme of special interest on this side of the Atlantic was the democratization of the Church, which had previously been perceived as a society sharply divided into rulers and ruled, teachers and taught. Vatican II brought about a wider distribution of power, by giving all bishops a share in the supreme government of the Church, rather than allowing them to be perceived as mere deputies of the pope. The council sought also to upgrade the status of the laity by authorizing pastoral councils on which the laity would have representation. In its revisions of the liturgy, a key principle was to increase the active participation of the laity, so that not even the sacrifice of the Mass could any longer be considered the action of the priest alone. David J. O'Brien, commenting on these developments, has said: "The stress on common Christian vocation exalted the dignity of the laity, asserted its responsibility for ecclesiastical decisions, and left the priest's role uncertain."[10]

In the United States, there was great concern for improving the relations between Catholics and other Christians. Here again, the council offered help. In its Decree on Ecumenism, it emphasized the possibility for a person to be a Christian without entering the Catholic Church, and, fur-

[9]Vatican II, *Dignitatis humanae*, no. 7.

[10]D. J. O'Brien, *The Renewal of American Catholicism* (New York: Oxford Univ. Press, 1972), p. 152.

thermore, asserted that non-Roman Catholic communities, as communities, have an ecclesial status and a real salvific value for their own members.

Although American Catholics were not greatly concerned about relations with most of the other world religions, relations with the Jews were of great concern in some parts of the United States. In this matter the council followed, on the whole, the guidance of the liberals. It firmly asserted that the Jewish people ought not to be held collectively responsible for the death of Jesus.

A major grievance of the liberals had been what they viewed as the monolithic centralization of the Church from Vatican I through the pontificate of Pius XII. On this point, too, the council seemed to offer relief. In its Constitution on the Church[11] and its Decree on Ecumenism,[12] the council stressed the value of having different customs and observances in different countries, suited to the variety of natural gifts and conditions of life. In its Pastoral Constitution on the Church in the Modern World, the council stated that each nation should develop the ability to express Christ's message in its own way, and that a living exchange should be fostered between the Church and the diverse cultures of peoples.[13] These principles were consonant with what Michael Novak was proposing when he wrote: "American Catholicism is becoming, and ought to become, different from any other form of Catholicism in history, because it is *American*."[14]

In its teaching on Church-world relationship, the council seemed to give official endorsement to the secularization that had been experienced in the previous decade by American Catholics. In many texts of Vatican II, the Church was depicted not as an end in itself, but as a servant in the transformation of human society in the pattern of the King-

[11] *Lumen gentium*, no. 13.

[12] *Unitatis redintegratio*, nos. 14 and 16.

[13] *Gaudium et spes*, no. 44; cf. no. 58.

[14] Novak, *A Time to Build*, p. 132.

dom of God. Mission was presented not simply as an effort to recruit new members but rather as the Church's commitment to the work of the Kingdom, and thus as including the restructuring of human society according to the gospel.

Another major problem for liberal Catholics in the United States was that of reconciling the Church's concern for continuity and tradition with the characteristically American desire for change and progress. In his references to the coming council, Pope John XXIII frequently spoke of *aggiornamento*, that is to say, "the adjustment of Christian discipline to the exigencies of modern day living."[15] In his opening allocution at Vatican II, Pope John stressed the importance of understanding the gospel message with modern tools of research and through what he called "the literary forms of modern thought." Following up on these directives, the Pastoral Constitution invited theologians to seek continually for more suitable ways of communicating doctrine to their contemporaries.[16] It also reminded all members of the People of God of their responsibility to take part in discerning the signs of the times and in assessing the many voices of our age in the light of the gospel.[17] Statements such as these seemed to allow for a dynamic and progressive understanding of the Church's teaching, accommodated to the American spirit of exploration and change.

3. Since Vatican II

Because of features such as these, liberal Catholics in the United States and elsewhere interpreted Vatican II as a victory for their own cause — one that had seemed all but lost only a few years before. The four years of the council (1962-65) were accompanied by a growing euphoria. Some American liberal Catholics spoke almost as though the parousia had arrived. But the council had hardly ended

---

[15]Pope John XXIII, *Ad Petri Cathedram* (1959).

[16]*Gaudium et spes*, no. 62.

[17]*Ibid.*, nos. 4 and 11.

when difficulties began to appear. Many of the bishops, on their return from Rome, seemed unaware of what they had done and were reluctant to implement what were being heralded by others as the conciliar reforms. Rome itself, while claiming to carry out the council, seemed to back away from the clear import of its decrees. The papal congregations reasserted their preconciliar powers and interpreted the documents of Vatican II, with the encouragement of the pope, in a highly restrictive manner. Pope Paul VI's encyclical *Humanae vitae*, prohibiting artificial contraception, was symptomatic of a much larger phenomenon.

Several reasons may be assigned for this official caution. For one, many adult Catholics, at least in the United States, were content with the Church as they had known it before the council. The supposed conciliar reforms threatened to deprive them of what had sustained their religious life and devotion since childhood. The liturgical changes had a particularly painful impact. Numerous American Catholics had been deeply devoted to the quiet low Masses of early weekday mornings, and to solemn Gregorian liturgies on Sundays and feast days. They were attracted to Benediction, Adoration of the Blessed Sacrament, private confession, the cult of the saints, and popular novenas. When all these treasures were suddenly swept away in favor of folksy guitar Masses, they felt cheated, bewildered, and distressed. Ecumenism and modernization, they protested, should not be allowed to destroy their beloved Catholic tradition. Understandably, church authorities were reluctant to upset their most faithful constituents any more than seemed inevitable.

Furthermore, the council documents themselves did not represent a clear victory for the liberal side. In every decree of Vatican II the conservatives had succeeded in safeguarding their own special concerns. For example, the Declaration on Religious Freedom deliberately "leaves untouched traditional Catholic doctrine on the moral duty of men and societies toward the true religion and toward the one Church of Christ."[18] The Constitution on the Church, while

---

[18] *Dignitatis humanae*, no. 1.

encouraging the participation of the laity, kept all real power in the hands of the clergy. It reaffirmed the prerogatives of the pope as defined by Vatican I — including papal infallibility — and gave the bishops practically unlimited power over all who were not bishops.

The Decree on Ecumenism, while expressing polite esteem for non-Roman churches, made no dogmatic concessions. It insisted that the Roman Catholic Church alone contained all the institutional features made necessary by Christ, and that it remained in that sense the only valid realization of the one Church of Christ. The Declaration on Non-Christian Religions carefully refrained from recognizing that these other faiths were based on divine revelation. Nor did it unequivocally absolve the Jews of Jesus' time from the crime of deicide.

The Constitution on Revelation insisted that public revelation had become complete in apostolic times, and that the magisterium of the Roman Catholic Church was alone competent to interpret that revelation authentically. All the council's words about the signs of the times and the sense of the faithful had to be understood in terms of this position.

Confronted by these facts, the liberal interpreters of the council came to admit the presence of strongly hierarchical and conservative statements in the decrees of Vatican II. George Lindbeck, for example, addressed this problem in the introduction to his *The Future of Roman Catholic Theology*.[19] After acknowledging the existence of compromises and deliberate ambiguities in the council documents, he proposed as the proper hermeneutical procedure that the new theological emphases be regarded as the most significant and that the old be understood in terms of the new, rather than vice versa. In this way he found it possible to subordinate many certain traditional teachings of Vatican II as incidental concessions to the conservative minority rather than central or emphatic affirmations. Yet it was possible for other interpreters to argue, with equal plausibil-

---

[19]G. A. Lindbeck, *The Future of Roman Catholicism* (Philadelphia: Fortress, 1970), pp. 4-5, 8.

ity, that in reaffirming the constant teaching of the Church throughout the centuries, the council was at least as author-itative as in opening up new directions for the present day. Even the innovations of Vatican II were for the most part retrievals of an earlier heritage.

As the liberal interpretation of the council was increas-ingly challenged, a number of progressives began to insist that the Church should move beyond the hesitant and ambiguous teaching of Vatican II. Inspired by the American dream, some radical Catholics developed specific programs, the general tenor of which can be summarized, without quoting chapter and verse, somewhat as follows.

In the name of religious liberty, all Catholics were consid-ered free to accept or reject whatever dogmas they found meaningful and credible, without blind submission to exter-nal authority. In the name of democratic equality, the resid-ual hierarchical elements in the Church were judged unacceptable. In place of a governing class perpetuating itself by cooption, the Church, it was asserted, should have freely elected representative leaders, accountable to the whole people of God.

In ecumenism, it was alleged, the council had stopped half way. A truly generous and open spirit, according to the radicals, required full recognition of the ministries and sac-raments of every Christian group, open communion, and the abandonment of any claim of special status on the part of the Roman Catholic Church. Similarly, according to this faction, non-Christian religions should be recognized as being on a par with Catholic Christianity, so that nobody should be urged to convert from one religion to another.

Pluralism in the Church, as seen by the radicals, required a major revision of the idea of papal supremacy. In place of a primacy of jurisdiction and personal infallibility, the radi-cal progressives advocated, through drastic reinterpretation of the conciliar decrees, what amounted to a mere primacy of honor.

Vatican II, these reformers held, had done well to broach the theme of the servant Church, but consistency, they added, would require that such a Church surrender all claims to superiority over the world which it served. It should humbly take its place as an equal alongside of secular humanitarian agencies working for the betterment of the world.

Finally, in its attitude to change, the council was accused of stopping short. Authentic modernization would demand that Christians listen to what God is saying today, and not simply repeat what God was believed to have said in the remote past. Talk of irreformable teaching and immutable dogmas, according to these progressives, was anachronistic in a world of rapid flux.

This program, which I have called radical, has perhaps never been explicitly formulated. It has existed more as a tendency than as a platform. But in the American atmosphere it would have been almost impossible for such a program not to exist. The American experiment, as currently understood, rested on implied dogmas such as self-determination, nondiscrimination, unlimited self-correction, equal opportunity for all, free election and public accountability of office-holders. Applied to the Church, these democratic dogmas involved the kind of program I have just sketched.

This radical revisionism was more vigorous in the late 60's, I would estimate, than it is today. It depended on two assumptions: first, that the American experiment had permanent and universal validity; and second, that Catholic Christianity could absorb this kind of change. Today, I suspect, many Americans are less confident of the democratic dogmas, because our national history has been, in recent years, a troubled one. Furthermore, the Catholic Church has shown unexpected resistance to this kind of radical reform. In some cases the reformers themselves, primarily intent upon social progress, lost interest in the Church and channeled their energies into secular causes, retaining only tenuous links with the Catholicism they had sought to revamp.

This thorough revisionism cannot claim to be warranted by the letter of Vatican II. In fact, it can be shown to run directly counter to the council's teaching on each of the issues in question. The council, while advocating freedom, emphasized the imperative to seek and adhere to the fullness of revealed truth and thus to the total heritage of Catholic Christianity. Vatican II, moreover, adopted a strongly hierarchical view of priestly ministry, with the bishops as supreme judges in matters of doctrine. It reiterated the teaching of Vatican I on the primacy and infallibility of the pope. It insisted on the unique status of the Catholic Church, as the sole possessor of all the institutional features made necessary by Christ. The council was therefore reserved in its teaching on mutual recognition and on intercommunion between the Catholic Church and other Christian bodies. In opposition to a purely secular understanding of the gospel, the council repeatedly stressed the importance of evangelization and conversion. All these emphases were contrary to the postconciliar radical agenda.

Do these and other "conservative" teachings of Vatican II run counter to the American experience? It must be admitted that Catholic Christianity as interpreted by Vatican II or any other council, has attributes markedly different from what Americans find congenial in their secular life. Whoever is convinced that the American political tradition of freedom, democracy, and reformability provides adequate norms for the Church will in time encounter serious difficulties in being a committed Catholic. Catholic Christianity cannot be governed from below by majority votes; it cannot allow its dogmas to be obliterated or reversed; it cannot absolve the faithful from their obligation to revere tradition and authority.

By acknowledging that values such as personal freedom, equality, and fraternity have a certain applicability in the Church, Vatican II made it easier for native-born Americans to feel at home with their Catholicism. If Vatican II had not shown a certain compatibility between the concerns of the American liberal tradition and those of perennial Christianity, there would have probably been more alienation and defection among American Catholics than in fact occurred in the late 60's and early 70's. But it is important, also, not to give the impression that the Church can be totally recast in the image of the American liberal society. There comes a point at which the Church must say that it is different from any secular society. Unlike any social, political, or academic institution, it is committed to the faithful transmission of a patrimony that comes from God by way of revelation.

The American experience of church, therefore, should not be simplistically patterned on the American political experience. Political experience of any kind cannot be made into a norm for judging the gospel. The gospel must be allowed to generate in the Church the special structures needed for the faithful transmission of the apostolic faith. A measure of conservatism is inseparable from authentic Christianity. Precisely in order to be a force for progress, the Church must adhere to the gospel originally given in Jesus Christ.

4. Conclusion

During the 1930's the United States passed through a period of doubt and disillusionment. The ideals upon which the nation had been founded seemed to be crumbling. Immigrant Catholics, who had found in this continent a place of freedom and opportunity, became the chief heirs of what William Halsey calls American innocence. Appealing to the order and rationality of the Thomistic synthesis, they helped to shore up the structures of the American heritage. During World War II and the ensuing cold war, Catholics became full partners in the shaping of American culture and public policy. From their national experience they were able to make a positive contribution to world Catholicism, as attested by the performance of the American bishops at Vatican II.

Since that time Catholics, together with other Americans, have experienced new trials and disappointments. The Vietnam War, the student revolts, the race riots, and the brutal assassinations of the late '60's, followed by Watergate, the Iranian revolution, the arms race, and worldwide economic depression, have sorely tested our national principles and goals. In the present crisis, Catholics are no longer naively self-confident. They have experienced bitter criticism and division within their own church. The aggressive, triumphal Catholicism of the post-Reformation period, severely censured at Vatican II, continues to decay. Chastened by the experience of their own fragility, Catholics are groping for a new identity.

Can American Catholics, then, find in their own tradition the resources demanded of them by the present situation? Vatican II, I suggest, may provide grounds for an affirmative response. In the judgment of Robert Imbelli, the major theological achievement of the council is to have broken the strangle hold of modern "traditionalism" by recovering a more ancient and dynamic idea of tradition.[20] Drawing on the "depth grammar" of this foundational reality, Imbelli is able to describe Catholicism in terms of its unique sacramental consciousness, bodily, communal, and historical. Other contemporary theologians have made similar assessments of Catholic roots.[21]

Catholicism, so conceived, offers a much needed corrective to certain less desirable traits of the American heritage. In place of religious privatism and individualism it unfolds the prospect of human solidarity encompassing a variety of cultures, times, and places. In contrast to the quantified universe of rationalism and positivism it proposes a qualitatively diverse world of symbol, sacrament, and mystery. Rather than worshiping the idols of self-fulfillment and success, Catholicism respects the discipline of failure and the fruitfulness of the Cross.

According to the astute sociologist of religion, Robert N. Bellah, the common good in the United States is currently threatened by an insidious combination of radical individu-

[20]R. P. Imbelli, "Vatican II: Twenty Years Later," *Commonweal*, vol. 109, no. 17 (Oct. 8, 1982), pp. 522-26.

[21]See, for instance, Richard P. McBrien, *Catholicism* (Minneapolis: Winston, 1980), pp. 1169-86.

alism and managerial manipulation.[22] Only a church with strong sacramental and hierarchical structures, resistant to individualism and sectarianism, can effectively oppose this threat. Catholicism has traditionally exhibited these structures and characteristics. It can make a much needed contribution provided that it does not allow itself to be weakened by the present tendency toward small, egalitarian base communities.

If Catholicism, inspired by its own best traditions, can do for America in our time something like what John Courtney Murray envisaged for it at midcentury, the Church will remain healthy and vigorous. It may be able once again to contribute significantly to the Church universal, as it did at Vatican Council II.

---

[22]R. N. Bellah, "Religion and Power in America Today," *Commonweal*, vol. 109, no. 21 (Dec. 3, 1982), pp. 650-55.

VATICAN II AND PROTESTANT SELF-UNDERSTANDING

George Lindbeck

Most Americans have probably heard some variant of the story of the army recruit who did not know what his religion was. He had never been to church or Sunday School, nor had his parents before him, and he did not believe in much of anything, not even God. He didn't quite know what a Jew is, and so he might be that, but of one thing he was absolutely certain: he definitely was not a Catholic. At this point the inducting officer interrupted him' "Well in that case," he said, "you must be a Protestant."

This is clearly an American story. It could not be told in a country of traditionally Catholic culture, and if by chance a somewhat similar anecdote were related there, the conclusion would be different: if you are sufficiently anti-Protestant, you are probably a Catholic.

The reason for starting our reflections with this pair of hypothetical tales is that they illustrate the interdependence of the notions of "catholic" and "protestant." A Protestant is what a Catholic is not, and a Catholic is what a Protestant is not. This principle reached its most absurd extreme in China where Catholic and Protestant missionaries selected different Chinese terms for God with the result that to this day many Chinese Christians (not to mention non-

Christians) think of Catholicism and Protestantism as totally distinct religions which even worship different deities, one named Shang-ti and the other T'ien.

Everyone is at least to some extent aware of how this logic operated in the pre-conciliar Roman Church (as it still does among traditionalists). Because Protestants believed in the priesthood of all believers, in bible reading, in religious freedom, and in the use of the vernacular in the liturgy, these things are clearly uncatholic. Protestants are, it seems to me, even more susceptible to this style of reasoning. As the decades turned into centuries after the Reformation, many beliefs and practices which the first Reformers had cherished were rejected as papist inventions. This happened to private confession, for example, and to the sign of the cross. Luther recommended both, and for a long time the churches influenced by him were basically medieval in these as in many other respects, but gradually this heritage eroded under the impact of anti-catholicism in both its protestant and rationalist forms.[1] By the nineteenth century, large groups in traditionally Reformation churchs were arguing that even the trinitarian and christological doctrines of the early church were catholicizing perversions of the original faith.[2] Or, to move from the sublime to the ridiculous, I know of at least one Lutheran congregation which continues to use the altar against the wall with the celebrant facing away from the congregation on the grounds that it does not want to imitate neighboring Catholic parishes.

In short, for four hundred years Protestants and Catholics have largely understood themselves in opposition to each other. One can even argue, as have some historians, that Western Catholicism did not become distinctively

---

[1] There is no comprehensive work which investigates this long decline in all its aspects, but the particular case of private confession is well-treated by Laurentius Klein, *Evangelisch-lutherische Beichte: Lehre und Praxis*, (Paderborn: Bonifacius, 1961.)

[2] The case for the centrality of these doctrines for the Reformation is discussed by Jan Koopmans, *Das altkirchliche Dogma in der Reformation*, (Munich: Kaiser Verlag, 1955).

"Roman" in the modern sense until after the Reformation.[3] We are, one might say, parasitic on one another; and especially a Protestant is by definition, as Samuel Johnson put it in the very first English-language dictionary, an adherent of those who "protested against the errors of Rome."

This, then, is the context in which I propose to look at the effects of the Second Vatican Council on Protestant self-understanding. My first thesis will be that the Council and its consequences are hastening the demise of Protestantism as a coherent religious and cultural phenomenon. This does not mean that the offspring of Protestantism are disappearing: they may now, as a matter of fact, be numerous in the Roman Catholic Church, and some of the most rapidly growing segments of Christendom are what we are accustomed to thinking of as Protestant sects. What is happening, however, is that once the glue of anti-catholicism is removed, historically Protestant churches are less and less unified in themselves and have less and less in common with each other. It has reached the point where, in most contexts, very little information is conveyed by calling a person a "Protestant." The term is, as a matter of fact, falling into disuse as a self-designation except when combined with a modifier as in phrases such as "Reformation Protestant," or "liberal Protestant," or "fundamentalist Protestant."

I have also a second thesis, however, which is more important. The logic of the Second Vatican Council's overall position, I shall suggest, is to exert a kind of cognitive pressure on what I have just called "Reformation Protestants" to become more catholic. To the degree that they become aware of the new possibilities introduced by the Council they are likely to think of themselves as Catholic exiles who now should be welcomed back into the Catholic communion, not despite but because of their Reformation heritage.

This, it must be emphasized, is not a general Protestant

[3]The term "Roman Catholic" was "originally used as a conciliatory term, in place of 'Roman,' 'Romantist,' or 'Romish,' early in the 17th c." *The Oxford Universal Dictionary*, Third Edition. (1944).

reaction to the Council, but applies to a specific group, albeit a crucial one. Before we speak of Vatican II, therefore, we must say more about the nature of Reformation Christianity, and how it relates to other forms of Protestantism. In doing this, I shall not so much be supplying readers with new knowledge as trying to organize information which everyone interested in religion in a place like the United States already to some degree possesses.

I

Protestantism as we know it today can be seen as a combination of three successive developments which are fundamentally distinct in principle even though the later ones partly grew from the first. The first of these developments is the Reformation itself. By this I refer to the so-called "magisterial" or "conservative" Reformation (in contradistinction to the "radical" or "left" wing) which is the origin of the three major Reformation churches or families of churches, the Lutheran, the Reformed (or, less accurately, the "Calvinist"), and the Anglican. It should be noted, parenthetically, that although most Anglicans do not consider themselves "protestants," they do not deny that they belong to a Reformation church, that Methodists are an Anglican off-shoot, and that most Protestant denominations which originated after the sixteenth century, such as the Baptists, the Disciples, or the United Church of Christ, come out of the Reformed side of the Reformation rather than from the left-wing. Thus with the exception of the "peace churches," such as the Mennonites and the Quakers, the great bulk of contemporary Protestant denominations go back in one form or another to the magisterial Reformation of Luther, Calvin, Zwingli, and Cranmer.[4]

[4]For details on the historical affiliations of various Protestant groups, see Arthur Carl Piepkorn, *Profiles in Belief: the Religious Bodies of the United States and Canada, Vol. II: Protestant Denominations*, (New York: Harper and Row, 1978).

This Reformation did not, in its first phase (and to some extent even in its second phase, as with Calvin), think of itself as anti-catholic. It was opposed to what it conceived as medieval corruptions and to the policies of Renaissance popes, but this opposition was for the sake of returning to the older catholic tradition in which, so it was claimed, the gospel of salvation through grace by faith as testified to by scripture was maintained. The Reformers thought of themselves initially as simply a reform movement within the Catholic Church of the West. They argued that they were good catholics who taught nothing contrary to the tradition of the fathers or even, as the Augsburg Confession of 1530 puts it, to "the Church of Rome in so far as its teachings can be gathered from its older and better writers."[5] For Luther, these "older and better writers" included someone as late as the twelfth century St. Bernard of Clairvaux whom he deeply admired for his writings on grace, but also, one may suspect, for his power to make and unmake popes, and his readiness to speak of a papal incumbent of whom he disapproved, Anacletus, as "anti-christ."[6]

The first Reformers, in short, did not think of themselves as founders of a new church, or a new form of Christianity. They insisted, furthermore, that they did not leave the Roman communion willingly, but were, rather, unjustly expelled. They were not even prepared to ordain their own ministers until the growing shortage of priests in the areas under their influence forced them to do so nearly two decades after the beginnings of the Reformation, and the church structures which they then established were from their point of view temporary and subject to dismantlement

---

[5]T. G. Tappert (ed.), *The Book of Concord*, (Philadelphia: Muhlenberg, 1959), p. 47. (The quotation is from the conclusion of the first part, the first twenty-nine articles, of the Augsburg Confession).

[6]A recent treatment of the relation of Bernard and Luther is E. Kleinedam, "Ursprung u. Gegenstand der Theologie...," *Dienst der Vermittlung* (ed. W. Ernst et al) (Leipzig: St. Benno Verlag, 1977), pp. 221-247. Bernard calls Anacletus "antichrist" in Letter 127. English translation in B. S. James (tr.), *The Letters of St. Bernard of Clairvaux*, (Chicago: Regnery, 1953), p. 188.

once the bishops were ready to grant what they called "freedom to the gospel."[7]

Needless to say, later generations of Protestants progressively forgot these emphases. Under the pressure of continuing polemics which reached their most intense form in the wars of religion, they increasingly ignored the pre-Reformation catholic tradition and tried to leap directly back over the millennia to the bible. The *sola scriptura* of many later Protestants was very different from that of the first period. Instead of asserting that the scriptural witness to the gospel is the center and norm of the tradition (the *norma normans non normata*), it more and more often came to mean that scripture should be the exclusive source of all Christian teaching and practice. It was not until nearly two hundred years after the Reformation that the famous slogan, "The Bible and the Bible alone is the religion of Protestants," was coined[8] (although admittedly many Puritans had antedated this slogan in their practice by several generations).

This second stage of protestant development, together with its pietist and revivalist accompaniments, is the source of the fundamentalism and conservative evangelicalism which is the folk-religion of protestant North America. There is much that is authentically Christian in this folk-religion but, like its Roman Catholic counterparts, it is subject to dangerous aberrations. It is present, sometimes massively present, in the mainline denominations, and is dominant in the so-called "electronic church." Its continuing power is astonishing, and presumably accounts for the

---

[7]The documentation for this paragraph is to be found in F. Haupt, *Der Episcopat der deutschen Reformation*, (Frankfurt a. M., 1863), P. Brunner, "*Von Amt* des Bischofs," *Schriften des Theologischen Konvents Augsburgischen Bekenntnisses* 9, (Berlin, 1955), pp. 5-77. In English, see H. Küng, *Structures of the Church,* (New York: Nelson, 1964), pp. 121-51, and A. Dulles and G. Lindbeck, "Bishops and the Ministry of the Gospel," *Confessing One Faith: A Joint Commentary on the Augsburg Confession by Lutheran and Catholic Theologians* (Eds. G. Forell & J. McCue), (Minneapolis: Augsburg, 1982), pp. 147-172.

[8]By William Chillingworth, *The Religion of Protestants, A Safe Way to Salvation* (1638).

fact that 44% of all Americans, according to a recent Gallup poll believe that "God created man pretty much in his present form at one time within the last 10,000 years."[9]

There is a third stage of Protestant development which is, for our purposes, even more important. This started with the rationalism of the eighteenth-century Enlightenment, and continued on in a different form in the theological liberalism of the nineteenth and twentieth centuries. Protestantism, partly because it was so divided, and partly because of the Reformation emphasis on personal faith and conscience, early came to favor religious toleration. It thus easily assumed the role of promoter of freedom of thought, of individual autonomy, and of innovation (or, as it was generally called, progress) in every sphere including the religious. In this way, protestantism became the bearer, and in part the origin, of the typical values of modernity. F. Kattenbush, writing eighty-six years ago in the most learned and prestigious theological reference work of the day, the *Realencyklopedie fur Theologie und Kirche*, says that these modern values are what protestantism had come to mean for the upper classes of English-speaking lands and of Europe.[10] The central concerns of the earlier stages of protestantism (the doctrine of justification by faith in Jesus Christ, and the emphasis on the bible) had receded or disappeared for most educated protestants, including many of the clergy, even while they continued to think of Luther, and to a lesser degree, Calvin as their heroes.

The protestantism which existed on the eve of the Council (and which exists today) is for the most part an amalgam in varying proportions of these three stages of its development. Even fundamentalism, for example, is in part a product of the Enlightenment. The very act of asking whether the "days" of creation in Genesis were twenty-four hours in length presupposes a modern scientific (i.e., Newtonian)

---

[9]News release Aug. 29, 1982 (Los Angeles Times Syndicate).

[10]"Protestanismus," Vol. XVI, pp. 135-182, esp. p. 136. This article remains perhaps the best extant examination of the development of the concept "Protestantism."

idea of time as an absolute rather than, as both Aristotle and Einstein in different ways agreed, a function of bodies in motion. Or, to state the same point more broadly, fundamentalists and Enlightenment rationalists have a similar notion of truth, and differ only on whether this applies to scriptural statements. Furthermore, the privatistic view of religion and the particular way of thinking about religious liberty characteristic of much Protestantism, whether liberal or conservative, have their sources in the third stage of development.

There is one combination of these stages, however, which is of particular importance for understanding Vatican II, viz., what has come to be called "neo-orthodoxy." This was for the most part a creation of theologians who, like Karl Barth, had grown up and been educated as liberal Protestants, but who, with the collapse of nineteenth-century optimism during the First World War, the depression, and the Nazi period, returned to the Reformation sources without by any means, however, entirely abandoning the achievements of modernity. They believed in democratic freedoms — indeed, were often socialist in their politics —and, without being rationalists, had no quarrel with modern science, and accepted Enlightenment standards of critical inquiry and intellectual liberty. They were largely quite uninhibited in their use of critical methods in the study of scripture and of church history, and yet they were orthodox, insisting on the supreme authority of the gospel message as attested to in the bible, on the basic correctness of the christological and trinitarian creeds of the early church, on the enduring value of the Augustinian doctrines of sin and of salvation by grace alone, and on the importance of the Reformation emphasis on justification by faith, not the works of the law. Their position, one might say, was a combination of modernity with Reformation Christianity.

II

This was the kind of Protestantism with which the progressive theologians at the Council who did most to shape its documents were chiefly concerned. These Catholic theologians had read the writings of the neo-orthodox, had sometimes studied under them, and had occasionally even composed books on them. They were well acquainted, in other words, with Protestant scripture scholars and theologians who to one degree or another seemed to be living proof that one could be both modern and also faithful to one of the mainstreams of historic Christianity, and if this is possible for Protestants, why not for Catholics? The books have yet to be written which document the neo-orthodox contribution to the overcoming of the Roman Catholic anxieties generated by the modernist crisis at the beginning of this century, but my own impression, partly based on my experiences as a Delegated Observer from the Lutheran World Federation during the first three sessions of the Council, is that the contribution was considerable.

Furthermore, many of the *periti* and some of the bishops, especially those from north of the Alps, were aware of how catholic the Reformation had originally been, and they believed the Reformation had been partly right. It had been largely right about the centrality of scripture, about the importance of personal faith in Christ, and even about the doctrine of justification — as Bishop Elchinger of Strasbourg informed the assembly in what for me was the most notable speech of the Council.[11] They thought, in addition, that the time had now come when it was possible to incorpo-

---

[11] This speech is to be found in English translation in Y. Congar, H. Küng, D. O'Hanlon (eds.), *Council Speeches of Vatican II*, (London: Sheed & Ward, 1964), pp. 143-146. The relevant passage on p. 144 is worth quoting:

"It is a certain historical truth that at the beginning of our divisions, those who took the initiative had no desire to act primarily and unconditionally against unity, but began by seeing that certain truths were fundamental in divine revelation; for instance, the apostolic rights of the Churches, in the schisms of the eleventh century, or again, in the sixteenth-century Reformation, the dogma of justification by faith in the Lord Jesus our Saviour, which had been defined at the First Council of the Apostles in Jerusalem. On the other side of the ledger, what scholar well versed in the history of those two periods would dare to doubt or deny that some Christians, perhaps many of them, and even Pastors of our Catholic Church, made light of these truths at that time (though they are certain truths) and sinned in various ways against those who bore witness to these truths?"

rate these emphases into Roman Catholicism; or, more precisely, to reintegrate these emphases into the catholic matrix in which they rightly belonged and in which they would regain their proper balance. This was the burden of a good many influential pre-conciliar writings, most notable, Louis Bouyer's *Spirit and Forms of Protestantism*,[12] and Hans Kung's *The Council, the Church, and Reunion*.[13] It is also reflected in Hans Urs von Balthasar's study of Karl Barth,[14] and even in a book, again on Barth, written by Jerome Hamer[15] who later, in his capacity as Secretary to the Congregation on the Faith, was deeply involved in the actions against Kung and Schillebeeckx. The same basic attitude is also clearly apparent in the works of the two theologians who were perhaps indirectly the most influential of all, Yves Congar and Karl Rahner. Although neither of them have written books specifically on Protestantism or Protestant theologians, they are insistent that various themes precious to the Reformers and neglected during the post-Tridentine period are vital to the catholic fullness of the faith.[16]

It is not surprising, then, that the final drafts of the Council's documents were written with great care to do justice to Reformation concerns. The official observers were well aware of this, not least because we were regularly consulted as to our reactions. It is even possible to point to specific wordings in some of the documents which originated in observers' suggestions.[17]

[12]Westminster, MD: Newman, 1956.

[13]New York: Sheed & Ward, 1961.

[14]*The Theology of Karl Barth*, (New York: Rinehart & Winston, 1971). (This book was originally published in German in 1951.)

[15]*Karl Barth*, (Westminster, MD: Newman, 1962). (The French original was published in 1949).

[16]For a comprehensive account of the background of this whole development, including a short section on Congar and some references to Rahner (see the index), see Paul M. Minus, *The Catholic Rediscovery of Protestantism*, (New York: Paulist Press, 1976).

[17]These instances are not as yet part of the public record, but, as P. Leviallain remarks, the status of observer "donnait peu de droits, mais permettait toutes les

At the same time, however, the final texts provide little explicit evidence of this desire to take account of Reformation emphases. Consider, for example, the stress in the Constitution on the Liturgy on cooperation or active participation by the worshippers. Vilmos Vajta has written that this is the point at which the Reformation concern for personal faith in connection with the reception of the sacraments is most apparent,[18] but the terminology is so different that perhaps only someone who, like Vajta, has written extensively on Luther as a liturgical theologian,[19] would notice the similarity.

The reason for the Council's reticence about fully acknowledging its attention to Reformation concerns is easy to understand. It is related to what we earlier spoke of as the tendency of Roman Catholicism and Protestantism to define themselves in opposition to each other. As a result, the conciliar reforms had to be presented as much as possible as based on *resourcement*, the return to the biblical and patristic sources, on the one hand, and on *aggiornamento*, up-dating or openness to the modern world, on the other. It was also safe to stress the importance of the Eastern Orthodox heritage. Reformation and later Protestant contributions, in contrast, were rarely labelled as such for that would have made it more difficult to mobilize the bishops in favor of the documents.

III

Let us turn now to the effects of the Council on Protestant self-understanding. Here, in order to save space, I shall make little effort to distinguish systematically between conciliar and post-conciliar developments.

---

influences, et souvent de facon plus efficace qu'une voix consultative de droit." *Le mécanique politique de Vatican II*, (Paris: Beauchesne, 1975), p. 145.

[18]"Renewal of Worship: De Sacra Liturgia," in *Dialogue on the Way* (ed. G. Lindbeck), (Minneapolis: Augsburg, 1965), pp. 101-128, esp. pp. 108-113.

[19]*Die Theologie des Gottesdienstes bei Luther*, (Stockholm, 1952) (published in abbreviated form as *Luther on Worship*, [Philadelphia: Muhlenberg, 1958]).

The most general effect has been to contribute to a weakening of Protestant identity which was already in process before the Council. Very nearly the only bond which held together the varieties of Protestantism on the eve of Vatican II was a shared fear of Rome, and even this was diminishing rapidly, at least in the United States, as is witnessed by the election of John F. Kennedy to the presidency. Perhaps that fear and dislike now remain strongest, not among religious Protestants, but among the more purely cultural ones whose values are simply modern, simply those of the Enlightenment. There continues to be truth in the adage that anti-Catholicism is the anti-semitism of secularized intellectuals, but this is less and less true of religiously-motivated Protestants.

Among Fundamentalists and conservative evangelicals, to be sure, there continues to be strong antipathy to Catholicism, but the old fear has largely vanished, in part because Rome is now officially on the side of freedom of religion, in part also because Roman Catholicism is no longer seen as a crushing powerful monolith, but as a tottering giant gravely beset by its own internal ills. It is, furthermore, not nearly so alien a giant. Even the most prejudiced are being induced by the mass in the vernacular, the greater christocentricism of worship as signaled by the diminution of extra-liturgical devotions, the change in garb of the religious and the clergy, the rise of the charismatic movement, the obvious presence in the Roman Catholic fold of many who qualify as "born again" even by revivalistic standards, and many other developments to acknowledge a surprising amount of what they can recognize as Christianity in the erstwhile "Whore of Babylon."[20] Lastly, conservative Protestants now find allies on the Catholic side for their favorite social crusades. Roman Catholics are no longer perceived as an immoral horde seeking to defeat the righteous cause of, for example, prohibition, but rather as among those with whom even a

---

[20] A good example of the changed attitudes is an editorial, "What Separates Evangelicals from Catholics," *Christianity Today*, Oct. 23, 1981 (XXV/18), pp. 12-15.

Jerry Falwell can unite in his Moral Majority. This conservative alliance between Catholics and Protestants is countered, on the other hand, by a progressive alliance on such issues as opposition to nuclear armaments. The situation is different, to be sure, in an occasional enclave such as North Ireland, but here in the United States, Protestants are not a solid bloc or even a loose confederation joined together in opposition to Rome.

One symptom of this, suggested to me in conversation by a church historian,[21] is that fewer and fewer people now use "Protestant" as a self-designation. Protestants describe themselves, rather, as fundamentalists, or conservative evangelicals, or charismatic, or some variety of liberationist, or as conservative, or liberal, or ecumenical Christians. This is a recent development: before Vatican II, only Anglicans and a few Lutherans avoided the self-referential use of "Protestant." Most of the groups which derive from the Reformation, furthermore, are well aware that they are closer to counterpart movements in the Roman Catholic church than to many of their fellow Protestants. What some people speak of as "radical" Catholicism,[22] for example, has the same features which I earlier ascribed to "modern" Protestantism.

In addition, however, to the contribution of the Council and its aftermath to a loss of oppositional Protestant identity, it has also added to the conviction of many modern Protestants that they are basically right. These Protestants believe there is no stopping the deluge once one acknowledges, as the Council has done, the claims of religious freedom, of critical inquiry into scripture, dogma, and the church, of relevance to the modern world, of the inevitability of pluralism, and of the need for ecumenism. They suspect that Roman Catholicism is now being stripped of its distinctive historic characteristics just as has already happened to much of Protestantism. It is becoming simply

---

[21] Professor John Stroup of Yale University Divinity School.

[22] See the paper by Avery Dulles, S.J., in this volume.

another denomination which is fated to participate willy-nilly in the creation of new forms of Christianity, and perhaps of religion as a whole. We are living in an era, they are convinced, which is not only post-Reformation and post-Protestant, but also post-Roman and post-Catholic. According to much of the conventional wisdom currently purveyed in the newspapers and in the academy, it is perhaps also a post-ecumenical age. What has happened, many would say, is the beginning of the final phase of the triumph of modernity, and the disappearance from the center of the stage of any and all major historic forms of Christianity. As you recognize, this description of the effects of the Council is very much the same as that of the traditionalists, except that what the Catholic traditionalists fear as a destruction of their identity, some modern Protestants welcome as an affirmation of theirs.

Those Protestants, however, who remain attached to the central emphases of the Reformation, albeit in an historically critical way, have quite a different view of the Council's accomplishments and therefore also of themselves. They think of the Council as having opened the gates, not to submergence in modernity, but to the recovery of the fullness of the Christian heritage: to the bible, to the early fathers, to the Eastern Orthodox, to the genuine achievements of the modern era, and to the sixteenth-century Reformation. It seems to them evident that Martin Luther would not be expelled from the contemporary Roman Catholic Church. The abuses which most aroused his fury have either disappeared or are no longer promoted by the authorities. My own guess is that a twentieth-century Luther would be opposed to current papal policies on clerical celibacy, and, I would hope, contraception and women's ordination, but not much else. He would probably regard John Paul II as not at all a bad pope, considering the impossible demands of his inhumanly difficult post. He would, I suspect, say that the pope ought to preach the gospel more and the law less, but he would also agree that the present Bishop of Rome proclaims the gospel more clearly than many, perhaps most, contemporary Protestant leaders.[23] For Luther, this last consideration would be crucial, because the gospel of God's unconditional love and unmerited promises in Christ Jesus was for him the center around which all his reformatory activity revolved. Perhaps I can sum up by saying that contemporary followers of Luther (and, as far as that goes, Calvin or Cranmer) are likely to be much closer on most theological issues to Cardinal Ratzinger[24] (despite his present position as head of the Congregation of the Faith) than to a fair number of Catholic progressives.

This openness of post-conciliar Roman Catholicism to what the Reformers meant by the gospel has resulted in a greatly increased appreciation among their present-day successors for the catholic dimension of the faith, for the importance of the visible continuity as well as unity of the church. The Reformers' sense of having been wrongfully ejected from the historic Western Church has begun to revive in recent years in this type of Protestant. Nineteen years ago while I was in Rome between the first two sessions of the Council, I wrote an article published in 1964 in the second issue of the *Journal of Ecumenical Studies*,[25] in which I suggested that those genuinely committed to the Reformation heritage should think of themselves as rather like a liberation movement, such as the Free French, at the end of the last World War. The Free French were exiles, but exiles who could consider themselves vindicated by the

[23]In this connection, the statement by Pope John Paul II on the Augsburg Confession on the occasion of its 450th anniversary is important, not least because it is the first time that Rome has taken official notice of this fundamental (and professedly catholic) Reformation document. The English translation is to be found in the July 7, 1980 *l'Osservatore Romano* (weekly English edition), and is reprinted in H. Meyer (ed.), *Lutheran/Roman Catholic Discussion on the Augsburg Confession: Documents* — 1977-1981, (Geneva: Lutheran World Federation [150 route de Ferney], 1982), pp. 59-61. See also the Pope's message of November 17, 1980 to the Council of the Evangelical Church in Germany, *ibid.*, pp. 62-66.

[24]Joseph Ratzinger's *Introduction to Christianity*, (New York: Herder & Herder, 1970), is a good example of Roman Catholic work which takes Reformation emphases seriously.

[25]"A Protestant View of the Ecclesiological Status of the Roman Catholic Church," pp. 243-270.

course of events. Yet once the oppressive policies which had led to their expulsion were repealed, they desired nothing more than to return to the homeland, not, if they were sensible, as rulers, but simply as participants in the life of the nation and in the task of repairing the damage done to themselves and to the mother country in the long years of separation. Like all analogies, this one falters, not least on the point that after four centuries of division the "motherland" for Protestants is not simply the Roman communion, but the ancient catholic heritage as a whole, including its representation in Eastern Orthodoxy. Yet after all the necessary qualifications have been introduced, the mood, the self-understanding, expressed in this similitude is now increasing in that minority of Protestants who are self-consciously and commitedly Reformation Christians.

To be sure, the notion of Protestantism as a liberation movement in exile has not been notably successful. It was taken up by the Lutheran theologian, Carl Braaten,[26] but was for the most part either ignored or rejected. In more modest formulations, however, such as the suggestion that Reformation bodies should regard themselves, not as distinct ecclesial forms of Christianity, but as a reform movement within the church universal, the same basic idea is met with growing frequency. It has been strengthened by the results of the interconfessional dialogues which have shown that the Catholic heritage is more evangelical, and the evangelical Reformation more catholic than most of us had previously supposed.[27] Some Protestants now prefer to think of themselves as "evangelical catholics" and, in good Reformation fashion, view their ecclesiastical structures as temporary expedients which can be terminated once the Reformation emphases are assured a voice in a reunited church. Such attitudes were particularly evident in the recent discussion of the possibility of the recognition by

[26]"Rome, Reformation, and Reunion," *Una Sancta* (New York) 1966, XXIII/2, pp. 3-8.

[27]See the successive editions of N. Ehrenstrom & G. Gassmann, *Confessions in Dialogue*, (Geneva: World Council of Churches, 1972ff).

Rome of the Augsburg Confession, the first major official statement of the Reformation position, as an expression of Catholic faith.[28] At times these attitudes even lead to a sense of outrage that Rome by its slowness in acknowledging the catholicity of Reformation Christianity is, not only harming itself, but also depriving Reformation Christians of a wider and fuller communion which is rightfully theirs.[29]

It is not the purpose of this paper to assign blame for this slowness. On the one hand, a candid Protestant self-assessment is bound to recognize that none of the churches which issued from the Reformation are in any consistent way evangelically catholic. When both heritages are strongly present, as among the Anglicans, they tend to be competitive rather than coinherent, and Roman hesitations, on the problematic assumption that this dissonance is their main source, may thereby be partially justified. On the other hand, it can be argued that if Rome were more positive or if it permitted national episcopal conferences to be positive, the cause of evangelical catholicism would be greatly strengthened outside as well as within the Roman Catholic communion. Perhaps it will take another Council, this time an even more ecumenical one, to make a decisive breakthrough on these problems.[30]

---

[28] H. Meyer, *op. cit.,* fn. 23 *supra* contains a selected bibliography. Esp. to be noted is Joseph Burgess (ed.), *The Role of the Augsburg Confession: Catholic and Lutheran Views,* (Philadelphia: Fortress, 1980).

[29] Such sentiments are, in my experience, generally expressed privately rather than in public and documentable form.

[30] For the need for another council to resolve contemporary Roman Catholic problems, see my "The Crisis in American Catholicism," in *Our Common History as Christians: Essays in Honor of Albert C. Outler* (eds. J. Deschner & K. Penzel) (New York: Oxford, 1976), pp. 47-66.

FAITH AND LIBERATION: DEVELOPMENT SINCE VATICAN II

Gregory Baum

Vatican Council II has been a turning point in the life of the Catholic Church. It is easy, in my opinion, to make a long list of the changes initiated by the Council. The Council recognized other Christians as Christians and other Churches as fulfilling a function in the divine plan of salvation; it relativized the self-understanding of the Catholic Church which no longer sees itself as simply identical with the Church of Christ; the Council recognized the presence of the Holy Spirit in the ecumenical movement; it acknowledged an echo of God's Word in the religions of the world and accepted humanity's religious pluralism; it came to a new appreciation of Jewish religion and freed the Church's teaching from the inherited anti-Jewish rhetoric; the Council tried to replace the monarchical by the collegial model for understanding the social organization of the Catholic Church; it recognized the priesthood of all the baptized and affirmed the participation of all Christians in the essential functions of the Church, implicitly raising a question mark behind the monarchical style of contemporary church government; the Council moved the Church from a static to a more dynamic self-understanding; the Council recognized God present in history as Voice and Empowerment touching the entire human family; it endorsed the "new humanism," in which human beings are defined above all by their joint responsibility for history and for one another; the Council affirmed the ideals of modern, pluralistic society and defended people's civil rights, in particular their religious liberty; the Council arrived at a new understanding of the Church's mission, one which takes into account the total range of promised salvation, including people's deliverance from oppression; the Council's emphasis on liturgy promoted a new spirituality beyond individualism, where worship becomes the joint surrender of the people with and in Jesus Christ to God's ever gracious design.

This list could, I think, be extended. The Vatican Council was a marvellous event, a *kairos*, an historical moment of grace and renewal. Yet what I want to examine in this paper is the emergence of a new orientation in the Church since Vatican II, an orientation that builds on the Council but that also significantly transcends it. I shall tentatively call this new orientation "liberationist."

Religious Experience and Biblical Warrant

The new orientation is grounded first of all in new religious experience.[1] Christians living under special historical conditions have experienced the divine Summons in their lives in a new way. One way of describing the new Christian experience is to say that it has joined faith and justice in an indissoluble way. The encounter with God in Jesus Christ makes people recognize that this God is on the side of society's victims. God is revealed as the God of love, but in a

---

[1]There is considerable literature on the new religious experience. For Latin America see the work of Segundo Galilea, "Spiritual Awakening and Movements of Liberation in Latin America," *Concilium* 89, pp. 129-38, "Liberation as Encounter with Politics and Contemplation," *Concilium* 96, pp. 19-33, and his Spanish publications, especially his *Espiritualidad de la liberacion*, Santiago, 1973. His work is introduced in English in A. T. Hennelly, *Theologies in Conflict*, Orbis Books, 1979, pp. 30-31. For the new religious experience in the USA see the work of Michael Crosby, *Thy Will be Done: Praying the Our Father as Subversive Activity*, Orbis Books, 1977, and *Spirituality of the Beatitudes*, Orbis Books, 1981.

society marked by oppression love manifests itself in justice. That faith had a love-dimension has always been recognized. Theologians spoke of *fides charitate formata*. Today the religious experience of many Christians caught in structures of oppression reveals that charity includes justice and that faith, fully formed faith, carries with it a justice dimension, *fides justitia formata*. This new religious experience differs from pietist experience which embodies the soul's encounter with God, the alone with the Alone, and hence excludes other people. The new experience enlarges the self and creates a new consciousness of solidarity, in which the others, especially society's victims, are present. The new religious experience is also different from the encounter with the sacred as the *tremendum et fascinosum*, described by Rudolf Otto. For in the new experience the sacred is the holy One who turned right-side-up the world turned upside-down by human sin. Faith and justice have here been joined in a lived experience.

In faith people receive the Gospel, accept God's judgement on a sinful world, acquire a new orientation toward society, and receive a vision of what social life is meant to be. Faith makes people critics of the present order. People suffering under grave oppression and struggling against it find in the Gospel message confirmation and hope. While the sinful world negates them, Jesus Christ affirms them. People who do not suffer under grave injustices but are in solidarity with society's victims hear in the Gospel God's judgement on social sin and God's promise of new, emancipated life. Conversion to Jesus Christ here means not only repentence of personal sins: it also means recognition and repudiation of the social sins pertaining to the society with which one is identified. Conversion resituates people in relation to their society and generates in them social involvement. The encounter with God in faith communicates direction and empowerment.

Who are the people who have had and who still have this new religious experience? They are, first, people born into subjugation now struggling for emancipation. They are, secondly, people who recognize this struggle for freedom and self-determination as the significant "sign of the times" and believe they cannot grasp the Christian message apart from this. Thus in Pope John XXIII's *Pacem in terris* (nn 39-43), the significant "sign of the times" to be understood in the light of the Gospel, is the freedom struggle of colonized peoples, of disenfranchized workers, and of women caught as they are in structures of subjugation. In his *Laborem exercens* (n. 1) Pope John Paul II also regards as an historical turning point the emergence on the political scene of groups, classes and peoples, formerly excluded from self-determination, who now struggle to free themselves. The Pope considers their struggles as the dynamic element of modern society. His encyclical promotes the solidarity *of* the workers (and the poor) in a joint struggle as well as the solidarity *with* workers (and the poor) on the part of those who love justice (n. 8). According to the encyclical, the Church itself, in fidelity to Jesus Christ, must be in solidarity with the oppressed struggling for justice. The Christians involved in emancipatory movements, then, are the ones who have had the new religious experience.

New religious experiences have a future in the church only if they stand up under the test of the Scriptures. Catholics tend to be reticent in regard to their own spiritual experiences. They realize how easy it is to be fooled by emotions. The Christians committed to emancipation found that their religious experience was confirmed by the Scriptures. God revealed Godself as on their side, in solidarity with them, giving them strength and direction. They did not look in the Bible for a few proof texts. They regarded the Scriptures as a spiritual criterion, a test that sorts out the human heart, a divine norm available not only to biblical scholars but more especially to the ordinary faithful.[2] The themes of the Bible that became very important to them were the Exodus as paradigm of salvation, classical Hebrew

[2]Many contemporary books treat the Bible in its totality as the record of God's call to justice: J. S. Croatto, *Exodus: A Hermeneutics of Freedom*, Orbis, 1981, J. D. Smart, *The Cultural Subversion of the Biblical Faith*, Westminster, Philadelphia, 1977, L. J. Topel, *The Way of Peace: Liberation Through the Bible*, Orbis, 1979.

prophecy, Israel's poetry of the good life, the messianic promises made in the Old Testament, the disturbing memory of Jesus as troublemaker and critic, friend of the outcasts of society, and preacher of the approaching kingdom, the logic of his persecution and crucifixion, the proleptic vindication of the faithful in Christ's resurrection, the eschatological promises, the apocalyptical images, and the persecution of the apostolic church by the Roman empire. These Christians speak of the dangerous memory of Jesus Christ.[3]

In much of Christian preaching and teaching, including the theological tradition, the Bible has been tamed. The subversive memories are left in the margin; and the passages that occupy the centre of attention are those that stabilize the present, integrate society, and summon people individually to greater love and holiness. Christians committed to an emancipatory struggle read the Scriptures from the viewpoint of the people at the bottom. They hear in the Bible a message that remains hidden from Christians identified with the successful classes, nations or races. In one of their pastoral letters, the Canadian bishops ask the faithful to reread the Scriptures to hear in it the divine summons to social justice.[4] Many familiar passages take on a new meaning once we read them from the new perspective. I read the Magnificat for many years; but it was only after my encounter with liberation theology that I heard its radical message: "God has put down the mighty from their thrones and exalted those of low degree; he has filled the hungry with good things and the rich he has sent away empty." The approaching kingdom rectifies society's sins.

The Christians touched by the new religious experience and confirmed by the reading of Scripture were in need of dialogue with theology. They looked for a critical clarification of their concepts. In fact, there were theologians com-

---

[3]The dangerous memory of Jesus Christ is a theme examined by J. B. Metz, *Faith in History and Society*, Seabury, New York, 1980, pp. 88-99, 200-204.

[4]The 1976 Labour Day Statement of the Canadian bishops, entitled *From Words to Action*.

mitted to emancipation who shared the new religious experience of faith-and-justice. They tried to clarify the meaning of the Gospel in the light of this new experience. They produced a critique of traditional theology and developed a new approach to theological reflection. Latin American liberation theology has become famous. Yet similar and parallel theological efforts have been made in other parts of the world, including the United States. What characterizes these liberationist theologies, and distinguishes them from traditional theologies, is their theory of knowledge. According to liberationist theology, action precedes the entry into truth, practice precedes theory, — or, more concretely, solidarity with the poor is the presupposition for the authentic grasp of the Gospel.[5]

Traditional theologies tended to be mainly concerned with people's personal lives. Sin meant personal transgression, conversion meant personal repentance, and grace referred to the transformation of persons. Liberationist theologies, on the other hand, reading the biblical message from the view point of society's victims, recovered the *social* dimension of sin, conversion and grace.[6] Sin includes the structures of oppression, conversion includes the raising of consciousness in regard to these oppressive conditions, and divine grace includes the Spirit-guided and Spirit-empowered struggle for a more just social order. Liberation be it economic, political or social, is then not simply a secular process: it is like all transitions from sin to justice 'supernatural.' Liberation is a movement produced by struggling people, sparked and sustained by divine grace. Liberation does not exhaust the meaning of salvation; at the same time salvation cannot be defined without reference to people's liberation from oppression.

It is not my intention in this article to examine the extensive theological literature produced by this new orientation.

---

[5]The most brilliant introduction in the new theological approach is Matthew Lamb, *Solidarity With Victims*, Crossroads, New York, 1982.

[6]Cf. G. Baum, *Religion and Alienation*, Paulist Press, New York, 1975, pp. 179-208.

What I wish to present instead is the extraordinary impact which this new orientation has had on the Catholic Church's official teaching. The new religious experience of faith-and-justice tested by Scripture, has led to a new life style in the Church and produced new theological reflections. At first church authorities were cautious: some episcopal voices even disapproved of the new orientation. Warnings were uttered against the politicization of the Christian faith. Yet there was also acceptance and approval. I wish to show that the impact of the new orientation on the Magisterium has been considerable. The new orientation *in* the Church is at a point of becoming a new orientation *of* the Church.

The Medellin Conference

Let me begin with the Latin American Bishops Conference held at Medellin, Columbia, in 1968, which was influenced, in part at least, by the new social justice orientation. In the Medellin Conclusions we find side by side, largely unreconciled, two distinct orientations to the problems of Latin America, one defined by the teaching of Vatican II, the other by Latin American liberation theology. It is useful for our purposes to analyse the difference between the two. Since the word 'liberation' has assumed such importance in Latin America, since it is biblically rooted and in keeping with Christian aspirations, the Latin American bishops have decided to adopt the word. They gladly speak of the liberation which Jesus brings. Christ is liberator. His truth shall make us free and introduce us to life in abundance. Yet the Medellin Conclusions contain two distinct meanings of the word 'liberation.' One of these I wish to call 'soft': it corresponds to a liberal, reformist understanding of social change and agrees with the perspective of Vatican II. The other could be called 'hard': it names the concrete conditions of oppression and implies a certain rupture or discontinuity with the prevailing order.

The soft meaning of liberation, found especially in the

chapter, "On Justice,"[7] refers to the transformation produced by divine grace in the lives of people: people expand in love, they are led into greater holiness, they are united more closely to God, they are more ready to make sacrifices, and as a result of these changes, they will build a more just society. Faith, hope and love issue forth into social justice. We are told that "authentic liberation" is "a profound conversion" to the way of God's reign. "The origin of the disdain of all mankind, of all injustices, should be sought in the internal imbalance of human liberty, which will always need to be rectified in history." We are told that "in the economy of salvation the divine work is an action of integral human development and liberation, which has love for its sole motive." Later we read that "we have faith that our love for Christ and our brethren will not only be the great force liberating us from injustice and oppression, but also the inspiration for social justice, understood as a whole life and as an impulse toward the integral growth of our countries." This is a reformist perspective in keeping with Vatican II. This understanding of liberation does not name the plague from which people suffer; it does not offend anyone because it does not specify the cause of injustice; it presupposes that the societies in question are capable of evolving toward greater justice. This 'soft' notion of liberation would not have given much consolation to the people of Israel under the rule of Pharaoh. The Israelites did not think that Egypt could be reformed; they wanted to be freed from the system of tyranny. Nor would this notion of liberation have given much consolation to the people of Israel during the Babylonian exile: the Israelites yearned for a radical change at the top so that they may be allowed to return to Jerusalem.

In the chapter, "On Peace," of the same Medellin Conclusions[8] we find the 'hard' notion of liberation. Here we are

---

[7]"Justice," Medellin Conclusions, in *The Gospel of Peace and Justice: Catholic Social Teaching Since Pope John,* edit. by J. Gremillion, Orbis Books, 1976, pp. 445-454. The subsequent quotations are taken from these pages.

[8]"Peace," Medellin Conclusions, in *op. cit.,* pp. 455-463. The subsequent quotations are taken from these pages.

told that injustices have created "a sinful situation" in Latin America. We move beyond the consideration of personal sins. There is structural sin, and unless we analyse and name it, we cannot see clearly, be converted to God, and wrestle against evil. The chapter mentions the twofold colonialism that oppresses the peoples of Latin America, first "the external colonialism" caused by the location of Latin America in the margin of the world capitalist system, and secondly "the internal colonialism" created by the extreme inequality between social classes, especially in countries marked by "a bi-classism," i.e. a small group of rich facing the marginalization of groups and peoples. According to the text, the internal colonialism in Latin America is derived from external colonialism: the class division is created by the dependency on outside powers, generated by the economic system and upheld by cultural and political forces. The text denounces imperialism as the enemy of human life in Latin America.

This 'hard' notion of liberation, drawn from Christians engaged in the struggle for liberation, analyses the concrete conditions of oppression, names the systemic cause of human misery, and signifies a certain rupture with the present order. The 'hard' notion of liberation inevitably offends some people, especially among the rich and powerful, and creates enemies for the Church. The 'soft' notion of liberation supposes that oppression in society is produced by sin, which in one way or another we all share, and hence must be overcome by the conversion of people from sin to grace, while the 'hard' notion of liberation considers reflections on sin in general or the sin in the hearts of people as an inappropriate analysis. It is necessary to focus on social sin, in the Latin American case on imperialism, colonialism and the structures of marginalization. These shall not be overcome by the entry of individuals into greater holiness, but if at all, only as the oppressed in solidarity wrestling together to overcome the evil system.

The difference between the two notions of liberation is considerable. Both have validity: which of the two is more relevant depends in part on the ethico-political judgement whether gradual reform is appropriate or whether people should struggle for more radical social change. The two notions also differ in the place they assign political commitment in people's lives. The soft notion of liberation presents the human person as growing in virtue and grace until at a certain point concern for society as a whole emerges: then political commitment is added to the wider quest for holiness. The hard notion of liberation presents human persons as caught in repressive structures beyond their personal choice, structures that affect every aspect of their being; thus personal growth becomes available to them only as they, in solidarity, struggle for emancipation. Here the political commitment is a basic dimension of the new being Christ offers them: it liberates all the other aspects of their personal lives.

Both notions of liberation have their validity; but they cannot both be applied simultaneously to people in the same situation. A choice is necessary. Often the people at the top come to different judgements than the people at the bottom. The ethico-political decision involved in this choice is in part derived from social scientific reasoning. Sociological analysis is indeed necessary to understand the structural inferiorization of groups and peoples. But the ethico-political decision does not depend on purely scientific insights. Social analysts using different sociological conceptual tools come to different sociological conclusions: hence the choice among different sociological approaches is crucial, and this choice is not a purely scientific one, but includes an ethico-political element.

The Canadian government, relying on the wisdom of their scientific advisers, has asked the Native Peoples to be patient, trust the government agency, and await the gradual transformation of their condition. If the Canadian government had hired theologians they would have proposed the soft notion of liberation to the Native Peoples. Politics is not everything, they would have said. Strive for personal growth and holiness; and then the time will come when you will even escape your present painful predicament. Yet the Native Peoples of Canada have lost their trust in the government; they have been deceived too many times. Since the structural marginalization inflicted on them affects every aspect of their lives, including the very formation of their consciousness from childhood on, their leaders have now opted for a more radical policy. They have made land claims which disrupt the legal system and the social peace of Canada. They struggle for radical social change. The Canadian Churches have decided to stand with the Native Peoples and support their claims. The theologians associated with the Churches present an interpretation of the Gospel based on the hard notion of liberation.[9]

The Latin American bishops gathered at Medellin in 1968, and at Puebla in 1979, were not united in their judgement which of the two notions of liberation would be more appropriate for the populations of their continent. That is why they inserted both notions in an unreconciled manner. Only subsequent history will decide which of these two notions will define the thrust of the Catholic Church on that continent. At the moment the Church is still divided.

Looking Back at Vatican II

Before continuing our examination of ecclesiastical documents, let us cast a glance at the teaching of Vatican II. The Council did not use the word "liberation." Still, the conciliar document, *Gaudium et spes*, significantly modified the Church's traditional stance toward society. *Gaudium et spes* affirmed modern society, albeit in a critical way. It affirmed the modern, industrial, technical, developmental society as the instrument through which justice could come to all people. "For the first time in human history, all people are convinced that the benefits of culture ought to be extended and actually can be extended to every one" (n. 9). Without weakening the primacy of the spiritual, *Gaudium et spes*

---

[9]For an analysis of the Native People's land claims and the involvement of the Canadian Churches, see Hugh and Karmel McCullum, *This Land is not For Sale*, Anglican Book Centre, Toronto, 1975.

affirmed the growth orientation of modern society, its global outreach, its quest for ever further development, even in remote areas which are as yet undeveloped. Vatican II asked Christians to engage themselves in social action. It criticized a purely individualistic ethics (n. 9). The holiness demanded at the present time includes concern for social justice and active participation in society. The Council recognized the emergence of "a new humanism" where human beings were defined primarily by their joint responsibility for history (n. 55). *Gaudium et spes* admitted that modern society was threatened by sin in many ways. It was tempted in particular to make its goods and achievements available only to a limited group of people and exclude others, especially the poor from the wealth produced (n. 29, 66). Here Christians, joined by others who love justice, should engage in the political arena and promote greater social justice. *Gaudium et spes* summons Catholics to universal solidarity. At the Council, the entire Church declared itself in solidarity with the human family. This shift was new and exciting.

Vatican II presented an optimistic view of modern society. It looked upon the modern world through the eyes of the reform-minded Christians of the developed, capitalist countries of the West. Influential in shaping the new teaching and progressive outlook of the Council were bishops and theologians from the successful European countries, Holland, Belgium, France, Germany, and Switzerland, supported on the whole by the bishops of the United States and Canada. These bishops and theologians, open, critical and reform-minded as they were, participated in the cultural optimism of the early Sixties. This optimism was grounded in the extraordinary economic progress that had been made in the West since World War II and supported by the expectation, confirmed by then current scientific theories, that this economic development could be exported to the less developed countries, the poor nations, until they would produce their own wealth. *Gaudium et spes* conveyed the impression that despite the selfishness of people, especially among the rich and powerful, there now existed networks of industrial, economic and political institutions that promised to lift the world beyond poverty and protect the freedom of persons. The first draft of *Gaudium et spes* submitted to the Council said very little of human sin. In the conciliar debate many bishops demanded that the Church's teaching on sin and the devil be introduced into the document. This was done. A special paragraph on sin was added (n. 13), which acknowledged the dividedness of the human heart, the human inclination to do evil, the abuse of freedom and the surrender of people to the lure of the Evil One. We find here not a single word about social sin! There is no reference to the structures of oppression in which people find themselves, which must be analysed, named, fought and eventually overcome. Vatican II affirmed the best of liberal society. Men of conscience should be able to steer the present, liberal, capitalist society away from exploitation and oppression so that it may become an instrument of justice and peace in the universe. While the word 'liberation' was not used, Vatican II actually endorses the idea of what we have called soft liberation.

In this context I recall a conversation I had during the Council with Paolo Ricca, an Italian Protestant, a Waldensian to be precise, who was a graduate student of New Testament, then acting as a journalist at the Council. (In the meantime he has become professor of historical theology at the Waldensian theological faculty in Rome.) We had become good friends. As I expressed my excitement with the conciliar draft of *Gaudium et spes*, he replied that for him the document was too much an endorsement of liberalism and liberal values. At the time, not being conversant with political science, I did not understand what he meant. I readily admitted that the Council promoted liberal values, especially the growth, unfolding, and self-determination of human persons under the impact of divine grace. This was to me a progressive step over against the former, more collectivist and authoritarian Catholicism, in which individuals were easily subordinated to the common good and the authorities that claimed to protect it. What I failed to see at the time, because my education had not acquainted me with the appropriate classical texts, was that this liberal notion of

the self-development of persons corresponded to the aspirations of the Western middle classes, but did not shed light on
the emancipatory struggles of people, including the working
class, who were structurally oppressed.

Turning Point 1971

The new liberationist perspective, partially acknowledged at Medellin, was recognized in the declaration of the
1971 Synod of Bishops, entitled *Justice in the World*. Over
the years the influence of third world Christian communities
on the administrative centres of the Christian Churches had
been growing. This was true for the World Council of
Churches, for the various world-wide denominational fel-
lowships, and for the Vatican, the centre of the Roman
Catholic Church. The Roman Catholic Church, more than
any other, is still firmly planted among the poor and dispos-
sessed of the third world and among the working classes in
many first and second world countries. In 1971, which I
regard as a turning point, two Roman documents, *Justice in
the World*, composed by the third Synod of Bishops, and
Octogesima adveniens, written by Pope Paul VI, adopted
the new liberationist perspective.

In the introduction to *Justice in the World*, the Synod
recognizes that there is being "built up around the world a
network of domination, oppression and abuses, which stifle
freedom and which keep the greater part of humanity from
sharing in the building up and enjoyment of a more just
world" (n. 3). The Synod acknowledges that over against
this system of domination has emerged among people "a
new awareness that shakes them out of fatalistic resignation
and spurs them on to liberate themselves and be responsible
for their own destiny" (n. 4). Where does the Church stand
in regard to this social conflict? "Listening to the cry of those
who suffer violence and are oppressed by unjust systems and
structures, and hearing the appeal of a world that by its
perversity contradicts the plan of the Creator," the Synod
affirms "the Church's vocation to be present in the world to

proclaim the Good News to the poor, freedom to the oppressed, and joy to the afflicted" (n. 5).

The system of domination of which the Synod speaks is undoubtedly imperialism and colonialism in its various forms, capitalist or communist, which inflicts oppression on sectors of populations. Over against these, the Synod sees liberation movements aiming at self-determination and self-reliant development. In this situation, if I understand the above text correctly, the Church takes the side of the poor and announces them the Good News of their liberation. This is 'hard' liberation: for the synodal text analyses the conditions of oppression, names the system of domination, takes sides in the conflict, and implies a discontinuity with the present order.

In the next paragraph the synodal document declares that the redemption Jesus Christ has brought includes "the liberation of people from every oppressive condition." Action on behalf of justice, we are told, is therefore "a constitutive dimension of the Church's proclamation of the Gospel" (n. 6). The paragraph acknowledges the new religious experience of faith-and-justice and the liberationist perspective that has emerged from it. The grace which Jesus Christ offers the world includes the empowerment that renders people capable of struggling for their emancipation. For this reason the proclamation of the Gospel is not confined to words; it includes as "an integral part" witness and action on behalf of justice. The synodal teaching represents a significant developement of doctrine.

This new teaching is not yet found in *Gaudium et spes*. The conciliar document recorded a doctrinal development that was the stepping stone for the new, more radical position. *Gaudium et spes* clearly affirmed that the grace of Christ was operative in the whole human famiy, that wherever people were, in whatever religion or even without religion, they lived a conflictual existence defined by the pull of evil on the one hand and the divine summons toward a new, more human life on the other. "Since Christ died for all men, and since the ultimate vocation of man is in fact one and divine, we ought to believe that the Holy Spirit in a manner known only to God offers every man the possibility of being associated with the Paschal Mystery" (n. 22). What was not said in the conciliar document was that this divine grace, this association with the Paschal Mystery, was concretely offered to people in their struggle for justice and peace. This is affirmed for the first time in *Justice in the World*: the redemption which Christ has brought includes the liberation of people from their oppression.

In the same year 1971, Pope Paul VI sent the letter, *Octogesima adveniens*, to Cardinal Roy, Archbishop of Quebec, President of the Commission on Justice and Peace. The letter represented a considerable shift to the left on the part of the Church's official teaching. I wish to mention three points made in the letter, the acknowledgement of socialism as an option for Catholics, a new, more nuanced approach to the phenomenon of Marxism, and the appreciation of the critical function of "utopia," an idea derived from the revisionist Marxist philosopher, Ernst Bloch.

In previous papal teaching socialism had been condemned without qualification. In *Quadragesimo anno*, published in 1931 during the great depression, this condemnation extended to the revolutionary socialism of the Communist Party as well as to the democratic socialism of the European social democratic parties. Socialism was simply out of bounds for Catholics. There were hints in the encyclicals of John XXIII and the social teaching of Vatican II that these condemnations were dated and had lost their meaning in the present. But *Octogesima adveniens* was the first papal document that faced the new situation squarely. The letter acknowledges that many Catholics have in fact become socialists: they have done this, we are told, not merely on the basis of pragmatic considerations but as a political step inspired by their Christian faith (cf. n. 31). They see in the turn to socialism the forward movement of history. In this context, Paul VI writes, it is important to distinguish between various kinds of socialism (cf. n. 31). Some socialisms are irreconcilable with Christian faith, for they are wedded to a total philosophy or world view that excludes Jesus Christ. But socialisms that remain ideologically pluralistic are acceptable. With this letter, Paul VI opened the door for Christians in third world countries to join the building up of their own African and Asian socialism. Socialism was no longer taboo.

While papal teaching in the past rejected Marxism as a single, monolythic phenomenon, *Octogesima adveniens* takes a more nuanced approach (cf. nn. 32-42). It distinguishes between Marxism as a philosophy of history, as a political movement, and as a form of social analysis. As a conceptual system of world interpretation, as we have seen, Marxism must be rejected: as political movement Marxism is identified with dictatorship and domination and hence must be rejected by Christians. The papal letter here refers to Leninism, the official Marxism of the Soviet bloc; it does not deal with the democratic origins of organized Marxism prior to World War One, nor with the return to this origin in the emerging Euro-Communism and other revisionist Marxist movements. As a form of social analysis, the letter tells us, Marxism has its usefulness. Many Christians, we learn, regard a Marxist analysis of society as a scientific method helpful for understanding the revolutionary potential of society. While Paul VI does not dispute this, he tells Christians that this method must be applied with the greatest care. Since there is a certain inner unity between these various aspects of Marxism, an uncritical confidence in Marxist social analysis easily leads Christians to where they do not want to go.

This more nuanced approach to Marxism is new in the Church's official teaching. After 1971 several national hierarchies have published pastoral letters dealing with Marxism in which they follow the approach of *Octogesima adveniens*. In a pastoral statement on Marxism, the French bishops added a fourth dimension to the three mentioned by Paul VI: they spoke of "cultural Marxism."[10] By this they refer to the impact of Marxism on philosophy, social science, literary criticism and the cultural self-

[10]For analysis of the French bishops' statement, see G. Baum, *The Social Imperative*, Paulist Press, New York, pp. 184-201.

understanding of people who on the whole do not regard themselves as Marxists at all. Cultural Marxism is a widespread phenomenon in France. Dialogue with Marxism, the bishops tell us, has affected Catholic theology itself. They offer an example of this influence. They claim Marx's discovery that labour, i.e. the organization of production, as a great impact on the formation of consciousness has been taken seriously by modern philosophy and theology. Human consciousness is no longer regarded as floating above the material conditions of life; consciousness always remains, however free and creative it may be, grounded in particular socio-economic conditions and hence reflects people's concrete historical circumstances. If we are to believe the French bishops, this insight has also affected Catholic theology.

Finally, *Octogesima adveniens* borrows from Ernst Bloch the radical notion of "utopia" and recognizes its usefulness for the presentation of Christian social teaching (n. 37). Paul VI realized of course that for most people the word "utopia" referred to an impossible dream that inhibits action. "The appeal to utopia is often a convenient excuse for those who wish to escape concrete tasks in order to take refuge in an imaginary world. To live in a hypothetical future is a facile alibi for rejecting immediate responsibilities." But "utopia" may have a different meaning altogether. Paul VI here introduced Ernst Bloch's notion: utopia is the vision of an alternative world which generates "the kind of criticism of existing societies that provoke the forward-looking imagination both to perceive in the present the disregarded possibilities hidden within it, and to direct itself toward a fresh future." We read that "utopia sustains the social dynamics by the confidence it gives to the inventive powers of the human mind and heart." If utopia refuses no overture, Pope Paul VI continued, then it can also meet the Christian appeal. Utopia breaks down horizons, it leads beyond the present system and every ideology. Utopia, according to Paul VI, fits well into the Christian understanding of the world's future. While not every dream of an alternative society exercises a utopian function, there are impossible dreams that are extremely practical: utopias initiate a realistic, scientifically verifiable critique of the existing order, they uncover the as yet hidden potentialities of the present and of past tradition, and they generate ever new imaginative patterns of reconstructing life in accordance with greater justice.

By integrating the Blochian notion of utopia into the Church's teaching, Pope Paul VI has made room for radicalism in Catholic social thought. While it is necessary to entertain reformist plans for the society to which we belong, i.e. the U.S.A. or Canada, it is equally important and possibly even more urgent to entertain the vision of an alternative society and to think, speak and act out a commitment to an America that shares its wealth and is organized in a participatory manner.

The Canadian Catholic Bishops

The shift to the left that has taken place in the Roman documents in 1971 has profoundly affected the social teaching of the national hierarchies in many parts of the world. This can be verified by the evolution of the social teaching offered by the American bishops. It is not my intention to do this in this paper. Instead I wish to document very briefly the shift to the left in the social teaching of the Canadian bishops. After 1971, the Canadian bishops joined with the other Christian Churches in the promotion of social ministry in Canada. Several inter-church committees were founded whose task it was to examine various sectors of social life from a social justice point of view, including Canada's relation to the third world. The reports written by these inter-church committees were received by the Churches and strongly influenced the stance which the Churches adopted vis-à-vis the Canadian government and the social problems of Canadian society. The Canadian bishops made use of the material supplied by the inter-church committees to prepare their Labour Day Statements and pastoral letters on social justice addressed to Canadian

Catholics. While a detailed analysis of the bishops' teaching would be worthwhile, especially on such issues as world hunger, unemployment, regional disparity, Quebec's right to self-determination, and the rights of the Native Peoples in the North, I shall confine myself to a commentary on a single document, the bishops' Labour Day Statement of 1976, *From Words to Action.*

From Words to Action suggests that the present economic system no longer serves the best interests of the majority of people. Why? Because capitalism widens the distance between the rich and the poor, especially between the rich and poor countries, and secondly because capitalism allows the control of resources and production to pass into the hands of an ever shrinking elite. The bishops ask for "a new economic order." The terminology, we note, is taken from debate at the United Nations. Why is the Church concerned about these issues? Christian faith in our own day, we are told, has come to include commitment to social justice.

How can the Christian community be faithful to this commitment? *From Words to Action* outlines several practical steps that Christians should take. The first one is of a religious nature. The Canadian bishops ask Catholics to reread the Scriptures to hear in them God's call to social justice. Sacred texts with which we are familiar may well reveal new meaning and power when we read them from a new perspective. Today the Church has learnt to discern in the Bible God's partiality for the poor and oppressed. Secondly, the bishops ask Catholics to listen to the voice of society's victims. The marginalized are able to tell us something important about our society which we could not discover if we only talked to our friends. If we confine our conversation to the middle classes, to people who belong to the cultural mainstream, we shall not arrive at a critical and truthful self-understanding. The cultural mainstream tends to disguise from people social sin and exploitation operative in society. The Native Peoples, the poor, the unemployed, women and the underdeveloped regions, the non-white groups — they all have a message revealing the truth about Canadian society. (In this context I want to mention that in 1967 the Canadian bishops said that French Canadians were a people and argued that no peace would come to Canada until their peoplehood was recognized and institutionally protected.)

As a third step, *From Words to Action* asks Catholics to analyse the historical causes of oppression in society. In one way or another, the various forms of marginalization are linked to the present economic system that excludes certain sectors of the population from the wealth of society. (In another Labour Day Statement, that of 1977, the bishops claim that to understand the causes of injustice in society "a Marxist analysis," if utilized in nuanced fashion, can be very useful.) Finally, *From Words to Action* urges Catholics to become politically active to help overcome the causes of oppression in society.

At the same time, the bishops recognize that only a minority of Catholics follow this new way of the Gospel, a minority called "significant" because it summons the whole Church to greater fidelity. The bishops admit that this minority is often criticized within the Catholic community, especially "by the more powerful and affluent sector." This remark suggests that class conflict produces tensions even within the Church. The bishops regard it as their duty to defend and encourage this minority in the Church. The perspective of *From Words to Action*, supported by several other Canadian episcopal statements is an instance of the liberationist perspective described in this paper. Here we have a minority emerging in the Church, a minority deeply marked by new religious experience, Christians for whom faith and justice are inextricably intertwined, who read scripture and ecclesiastical doctrine in a new light, who discover in them the transformative power of Jesus Christ, and who for this reason find themselves in solidarity with the poor and marginalized, see their own society from a new perspective, entertain the vision of an alternative social order and commit themselves to social reconstruction.

Pope John Paul II

This new orientation has been fully endorsed by the teaching of Pope John Paul II. Because of the Pope's conservative approach to a number of strictly ecclesiastical issues, the mass media have tried to convince us that he is a conservative, protecting the status quo and assigning a low priority to justice issues. The facts are different. In his social teaching, Pope John Paul II not only affirms the turn to the left of the Church's official teaching but carries it further to a significant degree. In this paper we shall cast a brief glance at two of his encyclicals, *Redemptor hominis* (1979), and *Laborem exercens* (1981).

In his first encyclical, *Redemptor hominis* Pope John Paul II introduced three ideas that confirm and promote the new radical orientation. The first has to do with the Church's mission. We are told that Jesus Christ in his redemptive incarnation has united himself in some way to every human being and that therefore the dignity of people is grounded in Christ's presence to them (nn. 8, 13). What follows from this is that the Church's protection and promotion of human rights is a service rendered to Jesus Christ (nn. 10, 11). The Church's social ministry has a christological foundation. In the past it was customary to distinguish between the "supernatural" or evangelical mission to preach the Gospel so that the world may believe and the "natural" or secular mission, secondary and subordinate to the first, to promote human justice on earth. Today the papal encyclical affirms, on the basis of recent doctrinal development, that the Church has a single mission, grounded in Jesus Christ, which includes at one and the same time the proclamation of the Gospel and the engagement on behalf of social justice. The two belong together. They have become as inextricably intertwined as faith-and-justice. The redemption promised by Jesus Christ includes the emancipation of the oppressed; and the proclamation of the Good News must be accompanied by action for social justice.

While Vatican II put considerable stress on the Church's social ministry, on the service the Church is called upon to render to the world, the conciliar texts still allowed a conservative reading which distinguished between the primary mission to preach the Gospel and a secondary mission, subordinate to the first, to serve the world. *Redemptor hominis* no longer allows this dualistic reading. The Church's mission is one and indivisible: proclamation and witness to justice.

Pope John Paul II has repeatedly demanded that priests not assume leadership positions in political organizations. Again, the mass media has interpreted this as if he wanted priests to be silent on political issues and restrict their preaching to strictly religious matters. This is a grave misinterpretation. For Pope John Paul II, the preaching of the Gospel includes demands for justice and witness to solidarity. He himself has acted accordingly, not only in regard to Poland but also in supporting national hierarchies, such as the Brasilian bishops, in their emphasis on the inseparable unity of faith and justice. While priests should not normally assume high office in political organizations, they are to be mediators of Christian faith and social teaching with its inevitably political thrust.

Secondly, *Redemptor hominis* developed the concept of "concrete man" (n. 13). There is no "man in general" neither is there a humanity in the abstract sense. There are only people existing in concrete historical conditions without which their suffering, their struggles, their aims and purposes cannot be defined. It is impossible to understand humans abstracted from these conditions. Man is always concrete. For this reason, the encyclical argues, God's gift of the Spirit offers people not grace in general nor new life as such, but new life in the precise conditions defined by their historical reality. Divine grace is therefore also concrete. When the encyclical proclaims the primacy of the spiritual in people's struggle for a truly human existence, including social justice, it does not designate the spiritual life as the first step to be followed by a second, namely active engagement; what the encyclical affirms is, rather, that the spiritual life is the interior dimension of people's efforts to live humanly in the world. Spirit is always concrete. Spirit is always incarnate, always empowerment to act in the world, always oriented toward the humanization of life. The encyclical's stress on the primacy of the spiritual is the repudiation of the reductionist understanding of a world-building process that leaves out the Spirit and interiority, whether this be in Western, technologically-defined capitalist projects of world development or in Eastern European, technologically-defined communist projects of constructing a new society. Unless the primacy of the spiritual be protected, world-building endeavors will only lead to human alienation. Concrete spirit defines the true nature of praxis. The Pope engages here in dialogue with liberation theology.

Redemptor hominis introduced into the Church's official teaching another idea, closely related to the new perspective. We are told that today more than ever "man is under threat from what he produces, that is to say from the result of the work of his hands, and even more so, of the work of his intellect and will. All too soon, and often in an unforeseen way, what this manifold activity of man yields is not only subject to alienation, in the sense that it is simply taken away from the person who produces it, but rather that it turned against man himself" (n. 15). We have here a reference to the classical Marxist analysis of the historical dialectics. The product of human labour stands over against the producer, not only, as Marx and John Paul II argue, because workers no longer own the work of their hands, but more deeply because the product acts according to a logic of its own, no longer in accordance with the intentions of the producer. The human task, therefore, is to reappropriate the product of human labour, i.e., to reassimilate and become subject to the industries and technologies they have produced. Marx argued that capitalism prevents people from reappropriating the works of their hands; Pope John Paul adds to this that the same is true of communism. Yet the Pope acknowledges that it is indeed the human task and vocation to become the subject of human history.

The most radical expression of what I have called the new orientation is Pope John Paul II's encyclical *Laborem exercens*. This is not the place for offering an analysis of the

papal document. I have done this elsewhere.[11] In the following pages I shall simply single out four points, made in the
encyclical, which reveal the radical orientation of Pope
John Paul II's social teaching.

According to the encyclical, the source of oppression and
injustice in the world and the threat to the peaceful co-
existence of nations is the unresolved conflict between capital and labour. Because humans constitute themselves by
labouring, the domination built into the economic system is
the principal cause of human degradation (n. 3). The rightful order, the encyclical argues, is the priority of labor over
capital (n. 7). The arguments with which John Paul II
demonstrates this fundamental principle are drawn from
rational analysis and historical experience (n. 12). Presently
the priority of labor is violated in the capitalist countries of
the West where capital is for the most part in the hands of
giant corporations, and it is violated in communist countries of Eastern Europe where the stateowned industries are
managed by a bureaucracy that seeks to enhance the political power of the communist state. The priority of labour
over capital means, according to the encyclical, that capital
must be made to serve labour, that is serve first the workers
employed in the particular industry, serve secondly the
improvement of the industrial machinery and finally serve
the entire labouring society. Justice in today's society is
defined by labour's priority over capital.

How can this justice come about? According to the encyclical, the agent of social change in our societies is the
workers' struggle for justice (n. 8). This struggle, based on
the solidarity of workers, must be suported by the solidarity
of all who love justice, including the Church itself. The
workers' struggle for justice is the dynamic element of contemporary society. This struggle, we note, is not in the first
place against the ruling class, the ruling class is not the
enemy — the Pope distinguishes his ideas from Marxism —;
the struggle of the workers is for justice, for the priority of

---

[11]See G. Baum, *The Priority of Labor: A Commentary on Laborem Exercens*,
Paulist Press, New York, 1982.

labour over capital, and only when those in power are unwilling to recognize the norms of justice does the struggle turn against them. We have here a Catholic version of "class conflict."

What would a just society, in which the priority of labour is observed, look like? The nationalization of the industries, however necessary at times, in and by itself does not guarantee the priority of labour. What is important about capital is not ownership but use. To assure the priority of labour, what will be necessary in the first place is the co-ownership of the industries by the workers who labour in them (n. 14). Eventually workers themselves must become co-responsible for industrial policy. Secondly, what is required is a planned economy to meet the needs for industrial policy of the entire population (n. 17). This planning should be done by an agency, not part of the government, made up by representatives of the classes, regions and industries of the country, in conjunction with govenment. Pope John Paul's socialism is characterized by a principle of de-centralization, the workers' ownership of the industries, and a principle of centralization, the planned economy: the tension between these two principles is seen as protecting personal freedom and pluralism.

Finally, in a brief paragraph, Pope John Paul II extends his radical theory to the third world. He argues that even in the underdeveloped countries where the masses are excluded from production and hence are workers only potentially, the dynamic element of society is the struggle of the poor for social justice. The Church must therefore preach the solidarity *of* the poor *with* the poor (n. 8). The encyclical endorses and even extends what the Latin American bishops mean by the Church's "preferential option for the poor." Pope John Paul II gives the phrase a more obviously political meaning. The Church itself, we are told, because of its fidelity to Jesus Christ, must be in solidarity with the poor struggling to remake society.

This concludes our survey of recent ecclesiastical documents. We conclude that there exists in the Church a new movement or orientation, sparked by the new religious experience of faith-and-justice, tested by Scripture, explored and guided by an appropriate liberation theology, and approved by a doctrinal development within the ecclesiastical Magisterium. While this new orientation was encouraged by the social teaching of Vatican II, it also significantly transcends it. It is even possible to contrast the liberal perspective of Vatican II with the more radical or liberationist perspective of the new movement.

The Future of the Faith-and-Justice Movement

The openness of Vatican II to the modern world raised the question in the minds of some Christians whether the biblical faith was not in danger of being assimilated to contemporary culture. These Christians felt that Vatican II did not define sufficiently the distance between Gospel and world. The new, more radical orientation in the Church puts greater emphasis on the gap that separates Christianity from the cultural mainstream. The new religious experience of faith-and-justice makes Christians be at odds with society. Here Christians regain a strong sense of what the Bible calls "the sinful world." They attain to a greater awareness of their own Christian identity over against the self-definition of modern society. All they have to do is to pick up a newspaper to know that they are Christians. They find themselves swimming against the stream, critical of "the wisdom of the flesh" taught at schools and universities, critical of the culture of injustice produced by contemporary society, at odds with the dominant ideology designed to legitimate an unjust and oppressive world.

What is the future of the liberationist orientation in the Church? What do these faith-and-justice Christians do? How do they involve themselves in society? This paper is not the place to examine this important question in detail. Allow me to make two brief remarks, both of which deserve longer and more systematic treatment.

The first remark is that the ethico-political thrust of the Gospel has two distinct though interrelated dimensions, the cultural and the political. If the cultural dimension is neglected, people become activists. Since activism does not question the dominant presuppositions, it tends to remain on the surface. The ethico-political thrust of the Gospel affects first of all people's consciousness and their cultural self-understanding. Since the present unjust society is legitimated by cultural symbols and cultural values (often even in the name of Christianity) and held in place by the taken-for-granted common sense mediated by the cultural mainstream, the new social justice Christians engage first of all in a cultural mission, which is then joined to involvement in political action. The struggle for justice has a cultural, intellectual, spiritual dimension. While Christians want to be active in political issues in their countries, not least among them opposition to the contemporary nuclear madness, they may also regard the raising of consciousness, the intellectual, educational, and spiritual apostolate, as their primary concern. Supported by the Church's social teaching, they will help people to decode the message of society, to resist the lies that pass for common sense in a sinful world, and to look upon their own country from the alternative vision of society, more in keeping with the divine promises.

The second remark I wish to make has to do with the minority character of the new movement in the North American Church. The Canadian bishops, we recall, reminded us that these Christians constitute only "a minority," albeit "a significant minority." Since Canada and the United States are on the whole closely identified with an economic system in which the important decisions are made in terms of the maximization of profit and power, it is not likely that the majority of North Americans, be they Christian or not, will assume a critical social-justice stance. The neo-conservative spirit which is presently penetrating into many levels of society, including the ecclesiastical, is generated by the true insight that commitment to social justice will demand a high price from North Americans. Many people who know what should be done in North America to create conditions of greater justice in the world, believe that the price will be too high. It would be a strategic mistake, therefore, to engage in an effort to transform entire institutions, i.e., to change the parish, the diocese, the Catholic college, the theological faculty, or the teachers' association. To engage in such endeavors at this time would only produce failure, bitterness and despair. We would become depressed and endlessly lament over pastors, bishops, presidents and chairpersons. Even bishops who share the new religious experience of faith-and-justice are unable to transform their diocese and their parishes.

What is of great importance, therefore, is to find an appropriate minority strategy. Relying on a theory of social change, derived from Max Weber, I have suggested that social change takes place through the promotion of countervailing currents.[12] The ruling structures are too firmly implanted to be modified: they are held down by society's own common sense. But the people who experience the existing system as oppressive are often willing to follow countervailing trends. These trends are sparked by new ideas and a new imagination that account for people's suffering and offer solutions to present problems.

Some of these countervailing currents may be irrational and blind, some may even be dangerous; others, on the other hand, may be based on a sound analysis, attract people, threaten the dominant structures and then be crushed by those holding power. Under certain historical circumstances, which are difficult to foresee, countervailing currents may converge, gain a certain power, and at a particular moment in time succeed in transforming the dominant structures. This theory of social change certainly sheds light on what happened to the Catholic Church at Vatican II: here several countervailing trends in the Church, the liturgical movement, the biblical movement, the ecumenial movement, and the lay movement, which had existed for several decades partly underground and often under the frowns of the hierarchy, were allowed by Pope John XXIII to come to the surface and influence policy-

---

[12]For a brief statement of Weber's theory of social change, see G. Baum, *Religion and Alienation*, pp. 170-174.

making at the top. The same theory can also be applied to understand social change in secular society.

What I propose, therefore, is that the liberationist orientation, well grounded as it is in religious experience, biblical assurance, theological reflection and ecclesiastical approval, promote countervailing trends in Church and society. While it would be futile to try to change entire institutions, it is effective to find a few people, a minority, dedicated to social justice within these institutions, organize them in small groups and centres, create networks between them and establish sets of communication with similar church groups and sympathetic secular organizations. While the various groups may be engaged in different tasks, some more educational, others more political, others again issue-oriented, the common network binds them together and gives them a sense that they are part of a new movement in the Church, possibly a new movement *of* the Church. Imagine for a moment that in a city there were five justice Christians in every parish, involved in local projects and joined in a lively network, what impact would such an active minority have on the Church and on the city! The advantage of this minority strategy is that it does not depend on the cooperation of those in charge of the institutions, even though their cooperation is of great consequence. Thanks to such a minority strategy, moreover, there is always something we can do. We are never caught in total impotence. We can always find others with whom to promote a countervailing current of social justice, knowing that this is not a waste of time, but a contribution that in the long run prepares significant social change.

Because the powers of injustice are growing at this time, I believe that the justice movement in the Churches will assume ever greater proportions. To counter the destructive forces unleashed by the two world systems and their clash, religion may be the only available resource. I foresee the rebirth of the old world religions, but especially the emergence of a radical Catholicism renewed by the faith in Jesus Christ as the compassionate protector of humans on this earth.

"THE CHURCH WOULD LOOK FOOLISH WITHOUT THEM" WOMEN AND LAITY SINCE VATICAN II

Francine Cardman

When asked about human progress and the prospects for change in history, Teilhard de Chardin used to reply with words to the effect that it was necessary to take a paleontologist's view of things.[1] In assessing the Second Vatican Council, we, too, would be wise to adopt the paleontologist's point of view and recognize how brief the interval has been between that surprising and lustrous dawn and this much duller and more difficult day. We would do well to consider the council itself and its after-effects in light of a longer succession of days than simply the last two decades or this twentieth century. To make even a preliminary assessment of the council and the segment of evolutionary time since its close in 1965 necessitates a backward glance at the nineteenth and even the sixteenth centuries in order to locate the council historically and to place the events and portents that have followed it in their wider context.

[1]Teilhard's outlook is clearly stated in "Some Reflections on Progress," in his *Future of Man*, transl. Norman Denny (New York: Harper and Row, 1964), 61-76. His description of the moral dispositions necessary for human advancement could serve equally well as a statement of the conditions for the full realization of Vatican II: "a great hope held in common" (72).

On this view, the nineteenth century dominates the middle distance of the landscape around Vatican II. The church's failure in that century, particularly during the long pontificate of Pius IX, to engage the modern world that was erupting all around it constituted one of the major agenda items for the twentieth century council. That earlier refusal is nicely characterized by the last of the condemned propositions on the 1864 Syllabus of Errors: "That the Roman Pontiff can and ought to reconcile himself and come to terms with progress, liberalism and the modern age."[2] In taking up the dialogue with modernity that Pius and the First Vatican Council had largely refused, Vatican II made it possible for the Roman church to enter the twentieth century, if not to reconcile itself with "progress, liberalism and the modern age." The way, of course, had already been paved in the years between the two councils, but Pope John's intentions and the second council's deliberations marked a symbolic entry into new terrain.

At the same time, the council should also be placed against the more distant horizon of the sixteenth century, where the long-simmering debate about the reform of the church dramatically boiled over after the monk Martin Luther entered into it. In that century, too, polemics quickly displaced dialogue as the Roman church refused further discussion and the Protestant movement rapidly differentiated into separate church bodies. Reform occurred, but within a broken church; on the Roman side, many of the serious issues raised by the Reformers were simply ignored. In reopening that aborted discussion, Vatican II made much of the sixteenth-century agenda of reform its own: Mass in the vernacular, communion in both kinds, renewal of religious life and priestly ministry, affirmation of the Christian vocation of the laity, are only the most obvious of the issues transposed from that century to this. More important than particular changes enacted by the council was the attitude of reform that gave rise to them and the re-visioning of the church and its relationship to the world that accompanied

[2]DS (34) 2980.

them. Here the nineteenth century discussion intersected with the sixteenth, bringing into relief another feature of the landscape of the 1960s and later decades that owed much to both: the entry of the Roman Catholic church into the ecumenical arena.

It is in the longer light, then, of this span of centuries and of the continuation of those interrupted conversations that I want to look at the work of Vatican II and the beginnings of the process of its reception. I begin with the council's redis-covery of the laity and its concommitant reevaluation of the relationship between church and world. From this context I will focus on three groupings of people within the church who have been significantly affected by the council and who have, in turn, influenced the course of post-conciliar devel-opments. These are: lay people in their relationships to the magisterium and to ministry; women from all areas of the church's life; and women in religious communities.

Laity, Church and World

"What is the province of the laity?" asked Monsignor George Talbot in the mid-19th century. His reply, typically British perhaps, but in line with most of the Roman hier-archy of the day, was to the point: "To hunt, to shoot, to entertain. These matters they understand, but to meddle with ecclesiastical matters they have no right at all." His contemporary, Father John Henry Newman, not yet either eminent Victorian or Cardinal, approached a similar ques-tion rather differently. In reply to the rhetorical query, "Who are the laity?" Newman thought it sufficient to observe that "The Church would look foolish without them."[3] In Newman's time the ensuing discussion proceeded mostly by way of controversy, with a particular focus on the

[3]Talbot's remark quoted by Charles Stephen Dessain, *John Henry Newman* (London: Thomas Nelson and Sons, 1966), 117. Newman's is reported in John Coulson, *Newman and the Common Tradition* (Oxford: Clarendon Press, 1970), 112, from a memorandum of Newman's.

dangerous notion of "consulting the faithful." An effort to settle the matter at the First Vatican Council by promulgating a dogmatic constitution on the church was halted abruptly by the annexation of the Papal States by Victor Emmanuel. At Vatican II, however, the wisdom of Newman's observation was reflected in the council's decision to begin its consideration of the mystery of the church from the whole people of God rather than from the hierarchy. By completing the work of Vatican I, which had only gotten as far as the papacy in its unfinished document, Vatican II in effect recognized how foolish the church had looked without the laity for nearly a century.

A new vision of the church was taking form at Vatican II, a vision that looked beyond the Roman rhetoric of the nineteenth century and, to a certain extent, past the polemics of the sixteenth century as well, to a biblically and historically renewed understanding of the nature of the Christian community.[4] The vision was not complete or unambiguous. It stands somewhat uneasily alongside older pictures of the church and often describes the new in the language of the old. For instance, in attempting to indicate the fundamental significance of the laity in the church, the council could only proceed by negative definition: the laity are "all the faithful except those in holy orders or those in a religious state sanctioned by the church."[5] But in affirming

---

[4]Documents relevant to this section on laity, church and world are: *Lumen gentium*, Dogmatic Constitution on the Church (LG); *Apostolicam actuositatem*, Decree on the Apostolate of the Laity (AA); and *Gaudium et spes*, Pastoral Constitution on the Church in the Modern World (GS). Quotations from *The Documents of Vatican II*, ed. Walter M. Abbott, SJ (New York: Guild Press, 1966). For a new translation which includes post-conciliar documents relating to implementation, see *Documents of Vatican II*, ed. Austin P. Flannery, OP (Grand Rapids, MI: Eerdman's, 1975). For an analysis of the council's vision and the tensions implicit in its ecclesiology, see George Lindbeck, *The Future of Roman Catholic Theology* (Philadelphia: Fortress Press, n.d.), especially chpt. 2, "The Church's Secular Mission." Avery Dulles, SJ, *Models of the Church* (Garden City, NY: Doubleday, 1974), further clarifies post-conciliar ecclesiology by distinguishing five basic models of the church in contemporary discussions.

[5]LG 31. See Ferdinand Klosterman, "The Laity," chpt. 4 of "Dogmatic Constitution on the Church," in Herbert Vorgrimler, ed., *Commentary on the Documents of Vatican II*, vol. I, 236-240, for a discussion of this definition; cf.

the common vocation of all Christians and their common call to holiness and mission by virtue of their baptism, the council recalled the insights of Martin Luther and the Reformers: "the layman's apostolate derives from his Christian vocation and the church can never be without it."[6] Much of the same mixing of perspectives can be seen in the ambiguous position of the laity that results from the council's juxtaposition of two very different images of the church in *Lumen gentium*. When the church is described as the People of God (or as a pilgrim church), it is clear that both laity and clergy are constitutive of its reality. But when the church is pictured as a hierarchical institution, there is no doubt that the laity take a secondary and subordinate place to the clergy. Despite its claims that the distinction between laity and clergy has a "unifying purpose," the council's identification of the clergy as the shepherds and the laity as the flock leads to a sharp disjunction between the clergy who guide and rule and the faithful "subjects" who follow them.[7]

Although the council sought to elevate the status of the laity and affirm that they were as essential to the church as the clergy and those in religious communities, it nevertheless retained a strong sense of the separation, if not the inequality, of the two groups by its stress on the worldly or secular character of lay life. Lay people are acknowledged to "exercise a genuine apostolate," but their activity belongs

Klosterman, "Decree on the Apostolate of the Laity," in Vorgrimler, *Commentary*, III, 305. Edward Schillebeeckx, "The Typological Definition of the Christian Layman According to Vatican II," and "A New Type of Layman," in his *Mission of the Church*, transl. N. D. Smith (London: Sheed and Ward, 1973), 90-116 and 117-131 is also useful.

[6]AA 1.

[7]LG 32 ("unifying purpose"). The shift in language and imagery from LG, chapts. I-II, the mystery of the church and the People of God, to LG, chpt. III, the hierarchical structure of the church, is striking. In the first two chapters, numerous scriptural images are used along with the image of the People of God; the word "flock" only appears three times, twice in the context of "little flock" as designating the whole church. In chpt. III alone, however, the word "flock" is used 14 times, and "sheep," "shepherd(s)" or the verb "to shepherd" appear 13 times, now clearly applied to a part of the church. I owe this insight into the predominance of flock imagery to Susan Costa, in conversation.

primarily in the secular realm, "penetrating and perfecting the temporal sphere of things through the spirit of the gospel." It is for the laity to "take on the renewal of the temporal order as their own special obligation."[8] In the many statements of this sort to be found in the writings of Vatican II, the church seems to exist as a reality apart from the laity, who are not so much themselves the church as representatives of it to the world. Only secondarily, it would seem, are lay people even thought of as being in the church, since their identity is so thoroughly shaped by their prior worldly location.

The reason for the council's emphasis on the secular character of the laity lies in its new-found regard for the world and the consequent need to maintain some tangible connection with it once claims to direct power over it had been renounced. By apparently accepting the world's "autonomy" and acknowledging the benefits that the church receives from the world, Vatican II signalled the end of the embattled relationship so characteristic of the nineteenth century and, to a certain extent, of each century since the sixteenth.[9] Yet, despite its positive — some might even say naive — appreciation of the world, the council could not conceive of church and world as integrally related. Instead, it had to resort to the laity as the link between world and church, so that the laity "consecrate" the world and "infuse it with a Christian spirit," while the clergy tend to the church, governing, teaching and sanctifying the faithful.[10] That the pattern of distinguishing church and world proposed at Vatican II should reflect and reinforce the contrast between clergy and laity is, therefore, not surprising.

Historically, two basic models of the church-world relationship have predominated in the church's life. In the first,

---

[8]AA 2 and 7.

[9]Joseph Komonchak analyzes the significance of Vatican II's recognition of the world's "autonomy" in "Clergy, Laity and the Church's Mission in the World," in *Official Ministry in a New Age*, ed. James Provost, Permanent Seminar Studies no. 3 (Washington, DC: Canon Law Society of America, 1981), 177-185.

[10]LG 34; AA 13.

the church maintains a critical distance from the world of which it is a part, respecting the world and desiring its transformation, yet never completely identifying with its claims and values. In the second model, the tension between the church and the world in which it exists is resolved into a social and political order that is at the service of the church or even dominated by it (e.g., medieval Christendom). Specific forms of relationship between laity and clergy correlate with each of the models. In the first, both laity and clergy constitute the church; each group is understood to be in the world, affected by it and concerned with it, yet equally distinct from it. On this model there is no ontologizing of the function of one group (i.e., the clergy) at the expense of the Christian and ecclesial status of the other. Rather an eschatological tension between the church and the world defines both groups, so that differences between them are relativized. On the second model, the eschatological tension is broken and the church dominates the world. Consequently, the lay-clergy relationship is made to bear the displaced weight of the church-world distinction. The broken tension between church and world is translated instead into tension between clergy and laity as the latter become identified with the world and the former with the church. The functions of each group are thus separated and ranked unequally, with the clergy filling a sacral and dominant role and the laity a strictly secular and subordinate one.

Considered in the light of these historical models, Vatican II's reevaluation of church and world looks more like an updating of the pattern of medieval Christendom than the creation of a new, self-critical understanding and relationship. Because, as Joseph Komonchak has so astutely pointed out, Vatican II lacked a sense of the political nature of human existence, it could not understand the church as constituted in and by, rather than in some sense prior to, the world.[11] As a result, the church remains in an important sense extrinsic to both the world and the laity. This leads to

[11]Komonchak, 185-190.

a fundamental lack of clarity which, I would argue, is at the base of many of the difficulties that have arisen since the council: papal objections to priests and nuns in politics, for instance, or the supposed "clericalization" of social action protested in the 1977 "Chicago Declaration."[12] For the same reason, the laity's surge of confidence after the council, their sense not only of what they could offer to the church but also of what they could expect from it, was often met by resistance on the part of their pastors. Conflicts serve the useful purpose of pressing toward clarification, even as continued theological reflection contributes new insights to practice. But it will take more time yet and further pressure before the ambiguities and tensions of Vatican II are resolved in the direction of a consistent interpretation and implementation. In the meantime, the energy and activity of various groupings of lay people are already influencing that future development, and it is to them that I now turn.[13]

Lay People: Magisterium and Ministry

Among the many areas of change and conflict since the council, two that have particularly involved lay people are their relationships to the magisterium and their growing interest and expertise in ministry. Widespread discussion, growing diversity, and open dissent in matters of sexual ethics characterize the first of these areas. Taken in conjunction with sweeping changes in social patterns, it is not

[12] Some recent papal remarks are cited by Komonchak, 169-170. The Chicago Declaration can be found in *Commonweal*, 105, 4 (Feb. 17, 1978), 109-116, along with several responses.

[13] Yves Congar, OP, has in many ways been the prophet and theologian of the laity's coming of age. See his germinal *Lay People in the Church*, transl. Donald Attwater (Westminster, MD: Newman Press, 1965), as well as his later reflections, "My Path-Findings in the Theology of Laity and Ministries," *The Jurist* 32,2 (1972), 169-188. Indicative of the new energy of the laity is the attention now being given to what is often termed (awkwardly, I think) "lay spirituality." See, e.g., Thomas Myott, "The Ecclesial Base of Lay Spirituality," *Spirituality Today* 32,3 (1980), 196-209; Dolores Leckey, *The Ordinary Way: A Family Spirituality* (New York: Crossroad, 1982).

surprising that this phenomenon has occasioned concern
for the institution of the family, particularly on the part of
the hierarchy. In the second area of change, lay people are
increasingly claiming an active role in the various ministries
of the church, official and unofficial, liturgical, social and
pastoral, and are not restricting themselves to those apostolic works which the council saw as particularly suited to
their secular calling. Because these are likely to be areas of
continued challenge and controversy for some time to come,
they deserve further consideration here.

1. Sexuality and Family

Issues relating to marriage, the family and sexuality have
been on the church's agenda, in one form or other, at least
since the Reformation. But they have been raised with new
urgency in the Roman Catholic church in the years since
Vatican II. The changing social roles of women and men, the
new economic conditions in both the developed and developing countries, medical advances, and evolving sexual
mores have all contributed to the climate in which church
teaching is challenged and sometimes rejected by lay people
(and often by clergy as well), even as it is defended and
reasserted by the hierarchy. Without attempting a comprehensive survey, I want to highlight several developments in
this area that bear on the larger issue of the laity as I have
raised it earlier.

The most obviously explosive issue in the years after
Vatican II was birth control and the widespread discontent
that followed upon *Humanae Vitae*, promulgated in 1968.[14]
Whether or not one agrees with Andrew Greeley's analysis
in correlating the decline of religious devotion in the United
States with discontent over birth control and papal authority, the fact remains that the birth control debate marked a
decisive turning point in the laity's sense of its own compe-

[14]Text in *The Gospel of Peace and Justice*, ed. Joseph Gremillion (Maryknoll,
NY: Orbis Books, 1976), 427-444. See also the Sacred Congregation for the
Doctrine of the Faith," "Declaration on Certain Questions Concerning Sexual
Ethics," in *Origins* 5,31 (Jan. 22, 1976), 485-494.

tence to make moral judgments in matters so intimately affecting their lives.[15] Catholic attitudes on this and other issues relating to sexuality have changed dramatically in the decades after the council.[16] For instance, in 1974 only 13% of all U.S. Catholics thought contraception was wrong, compared to 52% (not itself a high figure) in 1963. A 1979 survey of young Catholics in their twenties revealed that only 4% of that group believed contraception to be wrong. Similarly, in 1974 25% of all Catholics considered divorce wrong, compared to 46% in 1963, while only 11% of Catholics in their twenties in 1979 agreed with this view. Interestingly, the Catholic divorce rate has risen only slightly in recent years, from 15% in 1972 to 18% in 1980. Finally, 35% of all Catholics in 1974 (and only 17% of Catholics in their twenties in 1979) thought premarital sex was wrong, compared to 75% in 1963.

I cite these statistics not only to illustrate the extent of changing Catholic sexual mores, but also to call attention to a larger question about the relationship between experience and authority. In the nineteenth century Newman's notion of "consulting the faithful in matters of doctrine" was the subject of much controversy, and in the definition of papal infallibility offered at Vatican I, the pope's *ex cathedra* pronouncements on matters of faith and morals were judged to be irreformable "of themselves, and not from the consent of the church." Nevertheless, at Vatican II it was asserted that:

> The body of the faithful as a whole cannot err in matters of belief. Thanks to a supernatural sense of the faith,

[15]Andrew Greeley, *Crisis in the Church* (Chicago: Thomas More Press, 1979), 213-242. "*The birth control issue alone* seems to be the occasion for the substantial decline in religious behavior which has occurred among American Catholics since the early 1960's" (227). Richard McCormick surveys the effects of the birth control debate on ethics and theology in *Notes on Moral Theology 1965-1980* (Washington, DC: University Press of America, 1981), 215-231 ("The Encyclical 'Humanae Vitae'") and 768-785 ("'Humanae Vitae' and the Magisterium"). See also Joseph Komonchak, "'Humanae Vitae' and its Reception: Ecclesiological Reflections," *Theological Studies* 39,2 (1978), 221-257.

[16]Andrew Greeley, "A Profile of the American Catholic Family," *America* 143,8 (Sept. 27, 1980), 155-160. Subsequent statistics in this paragraph are from this article.

which characterizes the people as a whole, it manifests
this unerring quality when, "from the bishops down to
the last member of the laity," it shows universal agreement in matters of faith and morals.[17]

The development of doctrine is not the least of many inter-
esting questions raised by this text. But an even more
pointed question arises from the juxtaposition of this claim
with the statistics cited above. Might not nearly universal
disagreement in such matters of faith and morals suggest
that the disputed teaching is likely to be in error? Should
dissent on matters of sexual morality persist in time and
grow in strength, one can only expect that authority and
experience will be driven even further apart in the life of the
church, unless, that is, pastoral practice and formal teaching
find a way to acknowldge and integrate the insights of each.

Similar questions and possiblities are summoned up by
the 1980 Synod of Bishops, whose topic was the family.
Neither the bishops' gathering itself nor the Synod Secretariat in its preparatory work produced documents of particular distinction.[18] But the synod was, nevertheless, significant
for two reasons: the sociological and pastoral reflection
engaged in prior to the synod by many of its delegates and
episcopal conferences, and the way in which the question of
enculturation and particular churches was raised in numerous interventions from developing churches. Because of the
kind of pastoral attention given to the experience of the
laity, Archbishop John Quinn of San Francisco, then president of the National Conference of Catholic Bishops, could
make a remarkable intervention, in which he acknowledged
that extensive rejection in the United States of the church's
teaching on contraception "constitutes a profound theological and pastoral problem for the church," and called for new

---

[17]LG 12.

[18]For the Vatican Synod Secretariat's Working Paper, see the excerpt, "The 1980
Synod on the Family," *Origins* 10,15 (Sept. 25, 1980), 225-233; for the Synod's
"Message to Christian Families," see *Origins* 10,21 (Nov. 6, 1980), 321-325.

efforts to alleviate the crisis by the articulation of a more nuanced and holistic teaching on sexuality.[19] It was likewise out of the pastoral experience of the African church that Cardinal Laurean Rugambwa of Dar-es-Salaam could argue for a revision of marriage laws so that "a real Christian and African understanding of marriage and the family" could develop.[20] Even though the number of lay persons present at the synod was small, the proceeding made it abundantly clear that any future developments in church teaching, law and practice with regard to marriage, family and sexuality would have to occur in the context of pastoral practice and the experience of lay people.

2. Lay Ministry

One of the forces set in motion by the council was a growing pressure to rethink what had become the traditional Roman Catholic conception of priesthood and to subject it to the double corrective of historical understanding and biblical insight.[21] The influence of ecumenical interchange was also felt as Roman Catholic theology began to appropriate the Protestant terminology of "ministry" for its own reflection on the nature and meaning of priesthood. At

[19] "'New Context' for Contraception Teaching," *Origins* 10,17 (Oct. 9, 1980), 263-267. See also Archbishop Joseph Bernardin (then of Cincinnati), "Sexuality and Church Teaching," ibid., 260-262, in which he acknowledges the gap betwen church teaching and the attitudes of laity and even priests: "This constitutes a serious crisis for the church, intellectually, spiritually, and organizationally." The Synod also gave some attention to the changing situation of women and its effects on the other issues under consideration. See the intervention on behalf of the US National Conference of Catholic Bishops, in *Origins* 10,19 (Oct. 23, 1980), 299-301, and the remarks of Canadian Bishop Robert Lebel, "Oppression of Women: Sinful Situation," ibid., 302. Quinn's report on the synod to US bishops in *Origins* 10,23 (Nov. 20, 1980), 353-357.

[20] "Inculturation: The Communion of Particular Churches," *Origins* 10,20 (Oct. 20, 1980), 311.

[21] An early work of importance in this process was Yves Congar, OP, *A Gospel Priesthood,* transl. P.J. Hepburn-Scott (New York: Herder and Herder, 1967). Bernard Cooke, *Ministry to Word and Sacraments* (Philadelphia: Fortress Press, 1976), a thorough-going historical and theological study, has been extremely influential; now see also the recent work of Edward Schillebeeckx, *Ministry: Leadership in the Community of Jesus Christ* (New York: Crossroad, 1981).

the same time, the pastoral experience of the church was changing as a new form of ministry began to emerge: the ministry of the laity, whether as part-time volunteer or as trained professional. Considerable attention has been given to the growing phenomenon of lay ministry, and considerable confusion has attended the discussion as well.[22] The confusion has to do with both language and practice: which activities of the laity are properly considered lay *ministry*? how are such ministries recognized and made official by the church? must they be so validated? what is their relationship to the ordained ministry of the clergy? Some progress has already been made in sorting through these questions. As it continues, the significance of three related developments will become increasingly apparent.

The first is a linguistic shift that is likely to have far-reaching ramifications, as John Coleman has so persuasively argued.[23] The now pervasive use in Catholic circles —at least in circles of religious professionals — of the term "ministry" marks the rise of a "new ideology of church and status in the church." In this new language world, it is the laity who are the generic category for ministry; ordained ministers are only a particular instance of the ministry shared by all Christians. The conception of ministry represented by this view provides a powerful ideology for meeting the contemporary situation of declining numbers of clerics throughout the world:

> It is in the interest of the church, worldwide, to conceive of ministry in ways that undercut clerical caste...by substituting instead the designations of natural leaders of

---

[22]The most useful of the current crop of books and articles is David Power, *Gifts That Differ: Lay Ministries Established and Unestablished,* Studies in the Reformed Rites of the Catholic Church VIII (New York: Pueblo Publishing Company, 1980), and the essays in Provost, *Official Ministry in a New Age.*

[23]"The Future of Ministry," *America* 144,12 (March 28, 1981), 243-249. See also Maria Harris, "Questioning Lay Ministry," in Regina Coll, ed., *Women and Religion: A Reader for the Clergy* (New York: Paulist Press, 1982), 97-110, where she examines the terminology and its implications, while supporting the ministry of lay people.

a community for ministerial functions in the community.[24]

As the crisis of numbers becomes more acute, the promise of this broadened view of ministry will become increasingly obvious, not only in terms of meeting leadership needs, but also in discovering more appropriate modes of relationship and action between laity and clergy, church and world.

A second development is the increasing episcopal recognition of the changing sociological situation of the church and the consequent welcome extended by bishops in many parts of the world to the involvement of lay people in church activities of every sort. There is, in the bishops' growing openness to lay ministry, a new realism about the extent of the pastoral task confronting the church and the need for many new laborers for the harvest.[25] *Called and Gifted*, the statement of the American bishops on the fifteenth anniversary of the *Decree on the Apostolate of the Laity*, is a product of just such realism. In it the bishops speak in a new key as they "praise the Lord for what is happening among the laity and proclaim as well what we have been experiencing and learning from them." The concluding sentences of the brief document are perhaps the most noteworthy: "We have spoken in order to listen.... We now await the next word."[26] The bishops' new willingness to learn as well as to teach has much to do, I would contend, with lay people's new willingness to speak and to act.

Finally, a third development since the council is the evolution of a new category of minister alongside the familiar

[24]Coleman, 248.

[25]Some statements from bishops, diocesan commissions, or bishops' conferences worth noting include: *A Call to Ministry*, report of the Diocesan Council on the Priest Personnel Study Consultation, Diocese of Green Bay (Green Bay, WI, 1977); the pastoral letter of Bishop Howard J. Hubbard (Albany, NY), "We are His People" (Albany, NY, 1978); and the conclusions of the Asian Colloquium on Ministries, sponsored by the Federation of Asian Bishops' Conferences, "Ministries: Heralding a New Era," *Origins* 8,9 (Aug. 3, 1978), 129-143.

[26]NCCB, *Called and Gifted: The American Catholic Laity* (Washington, DC: USCC Publications Office, 1980), 1 and 7.

church volunteer and the more recent (and perhaps less familiar) lay liturgical minister who assists at Sunday Mass and sometimes in other pastoral situations (e.g., sick calls) as well. That new group is composed of the so-called "lay professional" who attended seminary or theological school and seeks a ministerial career in service of church and society. The American bishops have gone so far as to call this group "ecclesial ministers."[27] This appearance is further upsetting the structure of clergy-lay relationships already called into question by Vatican II. A caution should be noted in regard to this form of ministry: unless it continues to develop in the direction of ministries for justice and social change, as well as in the more traditionally pastoral ministries, it will run the risk of capitulating to an "ecclesiastical narcissism"[28] which concentrates almost exclusively on the internal affairs of the church. If, however, it manages to retain a broad range of understandings and functions, the development of lay ministry has the potential for transforming the Catholic experience of ministry and sense of church.

Not the least of the transformations one might expect from such a course of events is the creation of a broad base of ecclesial participation, so that women and men equally assume responsibility for the church's ministry and mission. And, indeed, movement in that direction has already begun, as women have claimed for themselves the vision of a new church at least implicit in the documents of Vatican II.

Women and the Council

Women appear in the council documents about as infrequently as they appeared at the council itself. No women attended the first or second sessions in any official capacity. In time this lack was noted and plans were made to include women among the lay auditors of the third session. The bureaucratic process of actually bringing women to Rome,

---

[27] *Called and Gifted* 5.

[28] Komonchak, "Clergy, Laity and the Church's Mission in the World," 193.

however, moved so slowly that, when Paul VI addressed a word of welcome to them at the opening of the session, there were no women in the auditors' section to hear him.[29] The *auditrices*, as they were so coyly called, arrived only gradually during the course of the third session. For the whole of the fourth, however, there were twenty-three women auditors present, working with commissions, speaking at press conferences, and otherwise following the council's proceedings.

Women are equally noticeable for their absence in the various decrees and constitutions of Vatican II. In discussions on the People of God or the laity in general, women do not appear by name. Although it is easier in Latin than in English to guess when *laici*, for example, is meant to include women as well as men, the problem of supposedly generic language is all too evident when one looks for the intentional presence and explicit inclusion of women in the documents of Vatican II. Where women do receive specific mention, it is almost always in the context of their role as wife or mother. I have only found three instances in which women appear in their own right — or at least not in the company of their husbands or religious communities.[30] Even there, however, the focus is on the social and economic progress of women rather than on women themselves. Discrimination against women — or, at least, discrimination based on sex — is of course among the various forms of discrimination repudiated by the council. I am not at all certain, however, that the "fathers" of the council expected women to take such statements of principle so directly to heart. The famous assertion of the fundamental rights of the person in *Gaudium et Spes* reflects a principle of justice

[29]Incident reported by Alice Curtayne, "The Council and Women," *Christus Rex* 20,4 (1966), 270. No mention of the absent women is to be found in the record of Paul's remarks at the opening of the third session (Sept. 14, 1964) in the *Council Daybook*, vol. 2, ed. Floyd Anderson (Washington, DC: National Catholic Welfare Conference, 1965), 5. In his statement Paul commented that "We are delighted to welcome among the auditors our beloved daughters in Christ, the first women in history to participate in a conciliar assembly."

[30]AA 9; GS 9; GS 60.

which women have since been pressing the church to apply
to its own internal life:

> ...every type of discrimination, whether social or cultur-
> al, whether based on sex, race, color, social condition,
> language, or religion, is to be overcome and eradicated as
> contrary to God's intent.[31]

One way to understand the significance of the current
women's movement is to see it as a call to the church — often
from outside it — to embody in its own life the principles of
equality and justice enunciated at the council. Out of this
ongoing dialogue of church and world, informed and
renewed by the church's reflection on the sources of faith,
and impelled by the concerns and experience of Christian
women, a new church is gradually being shaped.

In the years since the council, there has been growing
recognition at all levels of the church that the roles and
responsibilities of women within the church must expand
along with women's increased presence and responsibility in
the affairs of the world. Two important sources of change in
this direction have been the development of feminist theology and the presence of women in ministry. In both areas
Roman Catholic woman have benefitted from the experience of their Protestant sisters while also making their own
distinct contributions. It strikes me as not at all surprising
that some of the earliest and sharpest critiques of sexism and
religion have come from Roman Catholics — Mary Daly,
Rosemary Ruether, and Elisabeth Schüssler-Fiorenza, to
name only a few.[32] As feminist theology continues to articu-

---

[31]GS 29; cf. LG 32, where the indicative replaces the imperative.

[32]It is rather ironic to recall that Mary Daly began her journey to radical
feminism by earning doctorates in theology and philosophy from the University of
Fribourg. See her early article, "A Built-In Bias," *Commonweal* 81,16 (Jan. 15,
1965), 508-511, as well as her account of the process in *The Church and the Second
Sex*, with a New Feminist Postchristian Introduction by the author (1968; rpt. New
York: Harper Colophon Books, 1975); also *Beyond God the Father* (Boston:
Beacon Press, 1973). For Ruether, see "Is Christianity Misogynist? The Failure of
Women's Liberation in the Church" and "Mother Earth and the Megamachine,"

late women's experience, to press toward a theology that is whole, and to search for a more inclusive naming of God, the church will also change — either by broadening its experiential base, or by losing those women who are seeking new structures and relationships in both church and world. It is reasonable to expect that similar possibilities would apply to the experience of women in ministry as well. Leaving aside for the moment the question of women's ordination, it is clear that the presence of women in various ministries is already leaving its mark on the Roman Catholic church.[33] The fact that they are not ordained and have often come to ministry from the midst of the community means that women tend to approach ministry differently than do men.[34] The relational patterns and abilities that seem to be generally characteristic of women serve to reinforce this difference in ministerial style between women and men.[35] When the difference is joined with explicitly feminist

both in *Liberation Theology* (New York: Paulist Press, 1972); *Religion and Sexism* (New York: Simon and Schuster, 1974); *New Woman New Earth* (New York: Seabury, 1975), and *Sexism and God-Talk: Toward a Feminist Theology* (Boston: Beacon Press, 1983). Elisabeth Schüssler Fiorenza has written extensively on women in the New Testament church and early Christianity; her "Feminist Theology as a Critical Theology of Liberation," *Theological Studies* 36,4 (1975), 605-626, is an important theoretical essay; in addition to numerous articles, see *In Memory of Her: A Feminist Theological Reconstruction of Christian Origins.* (New York: Crossroad, 1983).

[33]For an early report, see M. Thomas Aquinas Carroll, "The Experience of Women Religious in the Ministry of the Church," *Chicago Studies* 13,2 (1974), 199-221. Data from an extensive study undertaken by the Center for Applied Research in the Apostolate (CARA) for the Ecclesial Role of Women Commission of the Leadership Conference of Women Religious is now available: *Women and Ministry: A Survey of the Experience of Roman Cathlic Women in the United States* (Washington, DC: CARA, 1980).

[34]I have explored an aspect of this difference in "Vocation Narratives," *Liturgy* 24,3 (1979), 25-30, drawing on the stories of Catholic women who feel called to priesthood, *We Are Called*, ed. Dolly Pomerleau (Rochester, NY: Women's Ordination Conference, 1978), and the report of a psychological study of women seeking ordination in the Roman church, *Called to Break Bread?*, by Fran Ferder (Mt. Rainier, MD: Quizote Center, 1978).

[35]Jean Baker Miller, MD, *Toward a New Psychology of Women* (Boston: Beacon Press, 1976), discusses characteristic differences and their social sources; Carol Gilligan, *In a Different Voice* (Cambridge, MA: Harvard University Press, 1982), analyzes the differences between women and men in regard to moral decision-making and moral development.

values (e.g., mutuality, participation, empowerment, shared decision-making), then the shape of ministry begins to change noticeably. One of the unintentional yet salutary effects of the inaccessibility of ordained ministry to Roman Catholic women is the new importance and form given to ministries once regarded as peripheral: hospital chaplaincies or pastoral care departments; campus ministries; ministries for justice. There is much promise for the future in this unexpected development.

Even so, change has been and will continue to be slow in coming. In addition to a predictable institutional reluctance to share the putative power (even the "power" of service) of the clergy with women and lay men, another force has worked to hold back change in personal and structural relationships between men and women. That force is the theological anthropology implicit in most of the council's documents and in later Vatican pronouncements concerning women.[36] The relation of the sexes presumed in this Roman anthropology might be characterized simply as "complementary but unequal." On this view, women and men are held to have clearly differentiated and God-given traits and qualities, so that there is not only a physical or biological distinction between them but also an ontological one. As a result, different spheres of influence and activity have been divinely assigned them; "progress" for women, whether in church or society, is limited to the assumption of "their full and proper role in accordance with their own nature."[37] There are signs that this position is weakening, but until it comes apart more or less completely, women will not be able to advance much further in their efforts to respond to the call they have heard in the winds of change raised by the council.

It would be a mistake to underestimate the impact of

[36]For an analysis of the texts until 1976, see Nadine Foley, OP, "Women in Vatican Documents, 1960 to the Present," in *Sexism and Church Law,* ed. James Coriden (New York: Paulist Press, 1977), 82-108. See also papal statements collected in *The Woman in the Modern World,* ed. the Monks of Solesmes (Boston: Daughters of St. Paul, 1959).

[37]GS 60.

women's issues on the church since Vatican II. On the American scene, for instance, Andrew Greeley reports that, "about one-third of young Catholic women may be said to be deeply disturbed by the church's perceived position on the role of women, and another one-third distinctly unhappy with it." From another survey of the attitudes of all American Catholic women, Greeley concludes that the problem is not exclusive to women in their twenties. Rather, one-half of Catholic women between thirty and fifty report having serious difficulties with the church's theology and practice in regard to women.[38] The church ignores alienation of this sort at its own peril.

The conflictual potential of women's issues increases when we turn to what is perhaps the most dramatic, and certainly the most visible, development since the council, the movement for women's ordination. That this is not solely an American issue — Roman protests to the contrary notwithstanding — can be seen clearly as early as the preparatory period for the council, when numerous Europeans addressed petitions and appeals on the subject to Rome. The St. Joan's Alliance, English in origin, carried its quest for the equality of women in church and society to the council as well, presenting it with resolutions calling for the ordination of women to the diaconate and presbyterate.[39] In the intervening years, the St. Joan's Alliance has gained international membership, as has the American-born Women's Ordination Conference (WOC). At its Second Conference on the Ordination of Roman Catholic Women, held in Baltimore in 1978, WOC highlighted the interna-

[38]Greeley, "Profile," 159, reports on both surveys.

[39]Eva-Maria Jung, "Women at the Council: Spectators or Collaborators?," *The Catholic World* 200,1199 (Feb., 1965), reports on these early resolutions and petitions. Partly in response to them and to other incidents at the council (such as the barring of a women journalist from communion at one of the council masses), Rosemary Lauer raised the question of "women's position" in "Women and the Church," *Commonweal* 79,13 (Dec. 20, 1965), 365-368. One of the early petitioners, Gertrud Heinzelmann, pushed the question further in "The Priesthood and Women," *Commonweal* 81,16 (Jan. 15, 1965), 504-508. Mary Daly's article exposing the "anti-feminist tradition" of the church and calling for the ordination of women follows Lauer's in the same issue ("A Built-In Bias").

tional dimensions of the movement with reports on the situation of women in the church and ministry by women from Mexico, Paraguay, Uganda, India and Belgium.[40]

Despite Roman efforts to quash the question, the movement grows. The Vatican Declaration on the Question of the Admission of Women to the Ministerial Priesthood, released in January 1977, is itself an admission of the seriousness of the issue.[41] Not only was a formal response deemed necessary, but the document itself took more than usual care to demonstrate that arguments for the ordination of women had been heard, considered, and, of course, met. An official commentary on the document was published, followed by a series of articles in *L'Osservatore Romano* further explicating its position.[42] Nevertheless, the Declaration was widely read and widely rejected. Refutations have run the gamut from a collection of more than forty detailed essays on particular points of the document to the dismissal of its basic premises by such noted theologians as Karl Rahner and Edward Schillebeeckx.[43] In the United States

[40]Texts of panelists' presentations in *New Woman New Church New Priestly Ministry*, Proceedings of the Second Conference on the Ordination of Roman Catholic Women, ed. Maureen Dwyer (Rochester, NY: WOC, 1980), 61-82. (See also: *Women and Catholic Priesthood: An Expanded Vision*, Proceedings of the Detroit Ordination Conference, ed. Anne Marie Gardiner, SSND [New York: Paulist Press, 1976].) Herve-Marie Legrand, OP, surveyed European as well as American literature for a state of the question report, "Views on the Ordination of Women," *Origins* 6,29 (Jan. 6, 1977), 459-468. For more recent instances of the ongoing international discussion, see the issue of *Lumière et Vie* 30,151 (1981) on the topic "Les Femmes: L'Église en cause," especially Marie-Jeanne Bérère, "L'Ordination des femmes," 90-102.

[41]Sacred Congregation for the Doctrine of the Faith, *Declaration on the Question of the Admission of Women to the Ministerial Priesthood*, with Commentary (Washington, DC: USCC Publications Office, 1977).

[42]*The Order of Priesthood: Nine Commentaries on the Vatican Decree Inter Insignores,* Our Sunday Visitor Sourcebook (Huntington, IN: Our Sunday Visitor, 1978). See also Louis Bouyer, *Woman in the Church,* transl. Marilyn Teichart (San Francisco: Ignatius Press, 1979).

[43]*Women Priests: A Catholic Commentary on the Vatican Declaration,* ed. Leonard Swidler and Arlene Swidler (New York: Paulist Press, 1977); Karl Rahner, "Women in the Priesthood," *Concern for the Church*, Theological Investigations 20 (New York: Crossroad, 1981), 35-47; Schillebeeckx, *Ministry*, 97. Reports from several other scholarly societies or commissions are significant;

one of the most encouraging signs of progress on the far from closed issue has been the two year dialogue between representatives of the Women's Ordination Conference and the Bishops' Committee on Women in Society and in the Church. In its report at the conclusion of the dialogue, the committee recommended that the Vatican Declaration be reviewed, that the church's teaching on woman as person be further developed and clarified, and that "significant levels of the church's ministry could be opened to women, perhaps including the diaconate."[44] Similarly, a number of U.S. bishops have written pastoral letters in recent years urging the participation of women at every level of diocesan life, the expansion and encouragement of the ministry of women, and the conversion of attitudes, structures and practices that have been neglectful of or hurtful to women.[45]

Pontifical Biblical Commission, "Can Women Be Priests?" *Origins* 6,6 (July 1, 1976), 92-96, concludes that scriptural data are inadequate to exclude women from ordained ministry (note: this predates the Declaration); Catholic Theological Society of America, *A Report on the Status of Women in Church and Society: Considered in Light of the Question of Women's Ordination* (Mahwah, NJ: Darlington Seminary, 1978), reports that "The Task Force does not, in sum, find that the arguments advanced on the question present any serious grounds to justify the exclusion of women from ordination to pastoral office in the Catholic Church"; and Task Force of the Catholic Biblical Association of America, "Women and Priestly Minsitry: The N.T. Evidence," *Catholic Biblical Quarterly* 41,4 (1979), 608-613.

[44]"The Future of Women in the Church," Report on the Dialogue between the U.S. Bishops' Committee on Women in Society and in the Church and the Women's Ordination Conference, *Origins* 12,1 (May 21, 1982), 8. See also "Dialogue on Women in the Church: Interim Report," *Origins* 11,6 (June 25, 1981), 81-91. The German bishops reach a similar conclusion with regard to the diaconate: French trans., "La Place de la femme dans l'église et la société," *La Documentation Catholique* 78, 21 (Dec. 6, 1981), 1071-1080.

[45]Most recently, these include: Archbishop Raymond Hunthausen (Seattle), "Pastoral Statement on Women," Oct., 1980, (Seattle, WA: Archdiocese of Seattle); Archbishop Peter Gerety (Newark), "Women in the Church," Feb. 26, 1981, *Origins* 10, 37 (Feb. 26, 1981), 582-588; Bishop Victor Balke (Crookston, MN) and Bishop Raymond Lucker (New Ulm, MN), "Male and Female God Created Them," Oct. 24, 1981, *Origins* 11, 21 (Nov. 5, 1981), 333-338; Bishop Matthew Clark (Rochester), "The Fire in the Thornbush: A Pastoral Letter on Women," April 29, 1982 (Rochester, NY: Courier-Journal, 1982), also in *Origins* 12, 18 (Oct. 14, 1982), 273-286. See also the *Task Force Report on the Role of Women in the Church of Southeast Wisconsin* (Milwaukee, WI: Catholic Herald, Dec. 6, 1982), published as received by Archbishop Rembert Weakland, OSB.

The question of women's ordination, then, will not go away, because the "women's question" will not go away. It will gain in importance, not because ordination is the final end of the women's movement, but because it is connected to so many other issues. As one of the signs of the times, its symbolic significance is vast. Women's ordination serves as a litmus test for the seriousness and authenticity of the church's commitment to justice and to the participation of all baptized women and men in its life and mission. It therefore raises again, in a particularly pointed way, the questions of clergy and laity, church and world which were examined earlier. It does this not only by asking how women are to share in the Christian call to holiness and ministry, but also by asking to what extent the church can and must listen to the world. The issues raised by the ordination of women are fundamental: how is the church to speak credibly to the world about the relationship between men and women, about family and social responsibilities, about justice, and about oneness in Christ? Can the church be the sign of a reconciled and renewed humanity that has been made a new creation in Christ?

Focused in this way, the discussion of women and the council goes beyond anything the council actually said about them, but it reaches to the heart of what the council was about. Hence, women have been putting some fundamental questions to the post-conciliar church. They have also begun to create new ways of being and acting in the church that reflect their commitment to a new sort of community. Among the women following this course are many members of religious congregations and orders, and even entire communities. In an earlier day these women might have prided themselves on their status as "religious" as distinct from "lay," but today are intentionally taking their place with their sisters — and brothers — among the laity.

Women in Religious Communities

"Women religious" has been the traditional identification

of this group of persons in the church.[46] As long ago as the
sixteenth century Martin Luther was critical of the distinction in status implied by designating one group of Christians
as "religious" in a way that set them off from others. Among
Catholics, the realization has grown since Vatican II that
both language and concept have failed to name and describe
adequately this way of life in the church. The distinction
between "religious" and laity has been at least as invidious
as that between clergy and laity; for women it has perhaps
been even more divisive than for men, since the clerical
option has not been open to them. Members of the church,
female or male, who follow this form of life in religious
community also experience the anomaly of their position as
something of a *tertium quid* in the church's constitution.[47]
Many of the men and, of course, all of the women are not
clergy, since they are not ordained. From the point of view
of theology, therefore, they should be counted among the
laity. Canonically, too, non-ordained members of religious
communities are lay people. But because of their particular
status they tend to share many of the privileges and restric-
tions applicable to clergy in canon law. Women's communities, especially those of cloistered nuns, it should be noted,
are subject to greater canonical regulation than are men's.[48]
The vows of both women and men set them apart from the
rest of the laity yet religious vows are often regarded as
distinctly second-best to the sacrament of orders. In terms

[46]The 1983 Code of Canon Law refers to Institutes of the Consecrated Life,
which are either Religious or Secular. The new language is awkward and the older
language of religious congregations and religious orders not only cumbersome but
outdated. I have settled on "women in religious communities" as an acceptable
circumlocution to avoid the difficulties (see text, below) raised by the term "women
religious." New language is needed here, as well as in regard to "lay" people, but it
will be some time yet in coming.

[47]Komonchak reveals something of this problem in his analysis of the two
different approaches to the clergy-lay distinction and relationship in Vatican II's
documents, "Clergy, Laity . . .," 171.

[48]See Richard A. Hill, SJ, "Religious," in *A Pastoral Guide to Canon Law*, ed.
George Dyer (Dublin: Gill and MacMillan Co., 1977), 106-122; the entire volume
was also published as *Chicago Studies* 15, 3 (1976); Lucy Vasquez, OP, "The
Position of Women According to the Code," *The Jurist* 34, 1/2 (1974), 131-137, for
women's religious communities.

of Vatican II's conception of the church-world relationship, members of religious communities do not take their identity as directly from the world as lay people are thought to do, nor do they represent the churchly realm as immediately as do the clergy.

Simply in naming and describing this group of women, therefore, our inherited language is inadequate. There are women who are "religious" without being either nuns or sisters, just as there are women who live "in community" (with, for instance, husband and/or children) without belonging to a religious institute. That the ambiguity of language and status is felt as keenly as it is today is one of the legacies of the council. It is thus somewhat ironic that the council's documents reflect almost no awareness of such semantic and conceptual difficulties. Yet I would suggest that the current linguistic impasse is a sign not only of lay people's raised self-consciousness, but also of the ferment which so-called "religious life" has undergone since the council mandated it the dual task of adaptation and renewal.[49]

Far more than their male counterparts, women's religious congregations have struggled to renew themselves in the spirit of the council. Their efforts have been intense and thoroughgoing, extending to structures, governance, ministries and mission. Often they have met resistance from curial officials charged with overseeing these communities and their implementation of the council's decrees. Conflicts between Rome and women's congregations are still commonplace today; there is every likelihood that controversy will increase rather than diminish in the future. John Paul II's exhortations to American nuns to wear identifiable religious garb is just one of many such skirmishes. While the habit may in itself seem a trivial issue, it is an issue that carries a definite symbolic weight. What is at stake in the

---

[49] *Perfectae Caritatis*, Decree on the Appropriate Renewal of the Religious Life (PC). The most important of the implementing decrees and instructions can be found in Flannery, *Documents of Vatican II*, particularly *Ecclesiae Sanctae* II (1966).

debate is not only Roman authority, but also an important aspect of the church-world relationship: how are nuns to be distinguished from lay women, their calling and way of life from the worldly pursuits of the laity, if they wear ordinary clothes? At the same time, however, it is ironic to note that wearing the habit is simply not an issue in 92% of American women's communities, though this fact seems to have escaped the notice of those who would enforce the pontiff's wishes in this matter.[50]

Even more significant for the church's future, as well as more alarming to Roman watchdogs, has been the direction most women's communities in this country (including those which are international in character) have taken in preparing new constitutions and renewing the structures of governance. In the overwhelming majority of American communities, as well as in most international institutes, the trend has been toward the creation of structures of shared leadership and participatory decision-making. This is so not only at the local or provincial level, but also at the level of national or international chapters.[51] Nowhere, perhaps, can this shift be seen more graphically than in the national organization of superiors of women's communities, the name of which has changed in the course of renewal from the Conference of Major Superiors of Women (CMSW) to the Leadership Conference of Women Religious (LCWR).

The effects of changes in structures and governance is a major topic of the Sisters' Survey of 1980, commissioned by LCWR as a follow-up to an earlier study they sponsored in 1967. In her preliminary report of the 1980 findings, Marie Augusta Neal, SND, makes several important observations about the changes that have taken place in the years between

---

[50]Marie Augusta Neal, SND, "The Sisters' Survey, 1980: A Report," *Probe* 10, 5 (May/June, 1981), 6: only 8% of the sisters surveyed affirmed the habit as a value.

[51]Neal, 4 and 6. See also her Paul Douglas Lectures for 1970, which analyze the early stages of this process of structural change: "The Relation between Religious Belief and Structural Change in Religious Orders," *Review of Religious Research* 12, 1 and 3 (1970-1971), 2-16, 153-164. For a report on the work of one institute, the Sisters of St. Joseph of Wichita, Kansas, see Cecilia Bush, CSJ, "A Total Participation Chapter," *Review for Religious* 38, 5 (1979), 734-741.

the surveys.[52] To begin with, she notes that morale today is much higher in local communities than it was in 1967, with 55% of the sisters surveyed reporting it to be better than it was five years ago, as compared to 35% so reporting in the earlier study. The data suggest that this boost in morale is the result not only of the assimilation of renewal, but also of the new structures of governance. 58% of those surveyed felt that renewal was proceeding at a good pace, compared to 42% in 1967. Perhaps the most striking evidence of a widespread change in attitude in regard to governance has to do with the desireability of having a local superior. Today only 34% want someone in charge locally, compared to 84% in 1967. Similarly, only 10% of the sisters surveyed indicated that obedience to a duly designated superior was the form of governance most congenial to themselves. Instead, various forms of participatory decision-making are the preference of a clear majority of the sisters, so that 64% of the respondents report that there is no longer any conflict about governance in their community. The constitutions of many groups reflect this new orientation, with 75% of them moving toward some form of shared decision-making. As Marie Augusta Neal pointedly remarks, "dependency is no longer the central religious value."[53]

A similar picture emerges in regard to the mission and ministry of women's communities. In their new constitutions, as in their mission statements, these communities are witnessing to a new-found sense of solidarity with the poor and a call to embody justice in the world, not only by alleviating suffering in immediate situations, but also by working for structural change that would root out the causes of injustice and oppression. For example, 62% of the sisters surveyed agreed that the church should have a primary focus on social justice, with 53% thinking that the church should act directly to alleviate the distress of the poor. Similarly 60% to 66% think that the church should

[52]Neal, "Sisters' Survey," for these and subsequent statistics.

[53]Neal, "Sisters' Survey," 5.

organize and act for justice nationally, whether alone or in collaboration with other churches. Action related to racism and issues of peace and disarmament is considered part of the church's mission by 64%, and 69% think that the church should act to address women's issues. In their own lives, and at every level of the community's organization, women in religious communities are embodying these new attitudes and commitments.

The far-reaching change in attitudes revealed in the 1980 survey represents the effect of new values, new structures and new ministries among religious communities of women. So strongly have these new attitudes taken hold that a small but growing number of women's communities are even willing to contemplate the possibility of no longer needing or wanting canonical status, should such status hamper their efforts to live out gospel values in the ways they have chosen. Whether occasioned by conflict over the revision of constitutions, or by other situations that might give rise to corporate dissent (as, for instance, in the operation of Catholic hospitals owned by these communities), the possibility of non-canonical status is entering the consciousness of many women's communities.[54] Needless to say, this is the stuff that curial nightmares are made of. Many of the unresolved issues of Vatican II will have to be addressed in this context as the discussion matures.

Looking back on the years since Vatican II, one figure emerges with special clarity for me out of the many persons, women and men, lay or otherwise, who have been moving the church forward in this time after the council. That figure is Theresa Kane, RSM, then president of the Leadership Conference of Women Religious, as she greeted Pope John Paul II at the Shrine of the Immaculate Conception in

---

[54]A rather surly exposition of the matter is given by Richard A. Hill, SJ, "The Community and the Option of Non-Canonical Status," *Review for Religious* 41, 4 (1982), 542-550. For a description of the kind of situation that evokes thoughts of the non-canonical option, see Margaret Farley, RSM, "Power and Powerlessness: A Case in Point," a contribution to a panel on "Women and Power in the Church," in *Proceedings of the 37th Annual Convention*, Catholic Theological Society of America, ed. Luke Salm, FSC (New York: CTSA, 1982) 116-119.

Washington, D.C., in October, 1979.[55] Her welcome to the Pope included a gentle but firm request that he be mindful of the "intense suffering and pain which is part of the life of so many women in these United States," who have been led by contemplation of the church's own teaching to seek a place in all the ministries of that church. In calling upon the Pope to "be open to and respond to the voices coming from women of this country who are desirous of serving in and through the church as fully participating members," she respectfully addressed him as one baptized Christian speaking in humility and charity to another baptized Christian about the pastoral needs of the People of God. For me, this moment was not only a welcome relief from the unrestrained adulation of the papal visit, but also a welcome glimpse of the future toward which Vatican II has set the church. In that simple and dramatic gesture, Theresa Kane became a symbol of all that has happened among the laity, women, and members of women's religious communities since the council.

The image of hope held in that picture was as bright an image as the one with which John XXIII opened the council:

> The Council now beginning rises in the Church like daybreak, a forerunner of most splendid light. It is now only dawn. And already at this first announcement of the rising day, how much sweetness fills our heart.[56]

I remain confident that the full light of that new day will, in time, break upon us as we struggle together to create a just church and a just world. But for now, we would do well some twenty years after Vatican II, to remember that it is still only a few hours past dawn.

[55]For the text of Theresa Kane's welcome and responses from several women theologians and church leaders, see *Women in Ministry: Response to Sister Theresa Kane and Pope John Paul II*, Theology in the Americas Documentation Series, no. 11 (New York: Theology in the Americas, n.d.).

[56]"Toward Christian Unity," address of Pope John XXIII at the opening of Vatican II, in *Catholic Mind* 60, 1168 (1962), 54.

AFTERWORD
Gerald Fagin, S.J.

"As Jesus was leaving Jericho with his disciples and a great multitude, Bartimaeus, a blind beggar, the son of Timaeus, was sitting by the roadside. And when he heard that it was Jesus of Nazareth, he began to cry out and say, 'Jesus, Son of David, have mercy on me!' And Jesus stopped and said, 'Call him.' And they called the blind man, saying to him, 'Take heart; rise, he is calling you.' And throwing off his mantle he sprang up and came to Jesus. And Jesus said to him, 'What do you want me to do for you?' And the blind man said to him, 'Master, let me receive my sight.' And Jesus said to him, 'Go your way; your faith has made you well.' And immediately he received his sight and followed him on the way."

(Mk 10:46-52)

The curing of Bartimaeus was no doubt a popular story in the early church. It remains an engaging narrative and an enduring symbol for the contemporary church.

The story portrays a group of people on a journey to salvation. Jesus and the pilgrims leave Jericho for Jerusalem, the place of salvation. Suddenly a voice cries out, "Jesus, Son of David, have mercy on me!" Through his persistent cries, the blind man is invited to come forward. In the space of a simple dialogue, he is led from blindness to sight, from darkness to light.

Bartimaeus was presented in the early church as an image of discipleship and prayer. He was aware of his blindness, of his need for healing. He persevered in prayer. His faith persisted despite discouragement. He responded quickly to the call of Jesus. We are told he jumped up and threw off his cloak. When asked what he wanted from the Lord, he asks only for healing, for faith. He wants only sight so that he may follow Jesus on the way. Bartimaeus dramatizes the call to join in the journey of salvation, a call to join the people on the way to Jerusalem.

In the years since Vatican II, we have become more aware than ever that we are people on a journey. Vatican II referred to the Church as a pilgrim people, the people of God who must continually follow Jesus on the way. To follow on that journey our eyes must be opened. Vatican II opened our eyes in startling ways to new horizons and a new vision of the Church in the modern world. It called us out of the darkness of our narrowness in relation to other Christians and other religions. It called us to see the wisdom and truth in other traditions and challenged us to be more faithful to our own. It called us to see the beauty of this world and its possibilities and challenged us to take responsibility for that world. It called us to see a new vision of the Church as a community of people, a herald of good news, a servant of God's Kingdom and all God's people and it challenged us to live as active and committed participants in that Kingdom. Vatican II opened our eyes in a new way to the basic Gospel message, a message of God's love and compassion and it challenged us to share that message with courage and enthusiasm.

The theologians in this book have challenged us to keep our eyes open and to continue to search for the meaning of Vatican II as it unfolds in the contemporary church. They have dealt with the major issues of the local experience of church, the ecumenical search for identity, the emerging role of laity and women, and the Church's developing consciousness of social responsibility.

The Document on the Church at Vatican II begins with the words, "The light of all nations." The Christian community strives to shed light and to bring the light of Christ into the darkness of the world. Like Bartimaeus, the new gift of light is only given so that we may more faithfully and generously follow Jesus on the way. The ultimate evaluation of Vatican II will not be in terms of new structures and ideas. The ultimate evaluation of Vatican II will be: Did it open our eyes to see Jesus more clearly? Did it deepen our conviction and commitment and trust in the power and presence of Jesus in human history? Did it make us prophets and servants in God's Kingdom committed to bring justice and peace?

Avery Dulles in *A Church To Believe In* has proposed that the dominant image of the Church is a community of disciples, a community of those who have heard the call of Christ and followed. It is not enough to be members of this community in some passive and minimal sense. It is not enough to fulfill obligations, perform duties, do what is required of us. It is not enough to be bound together by sterile assent to a creed and begrudging obedience. We are called to be disciples, followers of Jesus, committed to the Lord and committed to a vision of openness and compassion that is the mind and heart of Jesus, committed to a prophetic and hopeful vision that challenges the structures of prejudice and injustice in our world and makes us dedicated instruments of the coming of God's Kingdom.

In the light of the changes since Vatican II, we are confronted with a fundamental choice. We can say there has been too much confusion, too much uncertainty, too many questions, too many mistakes. In response we can close our eyes again and choose the comfortable darkness. Or we can open our eyes still more widely and follow the light wherever it leads, even if it means the way is less comfortable, less secure, less predictable. We must choose between fear that we rationalize as prudence and freedom that is founded in trust in God's Spirit.

We are a people on a journey. The years since Vatican II have taught us that it is a demanding but exciting journey. It has also taught us that there is still a long way to go. We like

Bartimaeus must be aware of our blindness, our need for healing. Like Bartimaeus we must persevere in prayer and faith. We must continue to cry out and never be satisfied with darkness. Like Bartimaeus we must respond quickly to the call of Jesus, and when he asks: What do you want?, our response can only be: "Lord, that we may see and follow you along the way."

49,373

DATE			
APR - 9 1980			
JAN 9 1991			
DEC 14 1995			
DEC 0 6 1995			
DEC 0 8 1997			
NOV 1 8 1997			
NOV 2 1 2001			
NOV 1 5 2001			